LEE CANTER'S

HOMEWORK WITHOUT TEARS FOR TEACHERS

Grades 4-6

A Publication of Lee Canter & Associates Inc.

Staff Writers
  Ann de la Sota
  Marcia Shank
  Jim Thompson

Illustrators
  Patty Briles
  Bob McMahon

Editorial Staff
  Marlene Canter
  Barbara Shadlow
  Kathy Winberry

Design
  Tom Winberry
  Bob Winberry

© 1988 Lee Canter & Associates Inc.
P.O. Box 2113, Santa Monica, CA 90406

ISBN 0-939007-16-9

Printed in the United States of America
First printing August 1988; Second printing February 1989

CONTENTS

PREFACE

To establish the best possible environment for teaching and learning in school, we at Lee Canter & Associates have developed a complete behavior management system— for teachers, administrators, support staff and parents. Our program, Assertive Discipline, has made a dramatic difference, nationwide, in the education of children.

In working with teachers over the years to solve behavior problems in school, we saw one issue surface again and again: problems with homework. Recently, Gallup Poll statistics showed that the most frequently recurring problem in school is the subject of homework.

To succeed in school, students must be able to do homework, and do it well. In our Homework Without Tears program, we're dedicated to helping them do that. In *Homework Without Tears for Teachers,* we'll show you your part in the homework process, and just how you can help your students achieve success.

Chapter 1
HOMEWORK WITHOUT TEARS

With homework, more is not necessarily better. As a matter of fact, unless homework is effective, we'd be better off without it. Homework that causes frustration and tears is much worse than no homework at all.

Lee Canter

If you are reading this, you care about making your homework assignments as effective as possible. And for good reason.

More teachers are assigning more homework in more grades than ever before. Many districts are adopting guidelines requiring teachers to give regular homework assignments. But why exactly is homework assigned? If you have never asked yourself that question, you should.

You may believe, as many educators do, that homework can reinforce what you teach in the classroom, help to individualize your instruction, improve student performance, help students develop effective study habits and provide an important day-to-day link between home and school. Many researchers agree that effective homework can do all of this and more.

But have you ever thought of the negative impact homework can have when it is not effective?

If your students are frustrated because they can't do homework, they will end up in tears. If parents are upset because homework means nightly battles with their children, they may be in tears. And if you end up correcting mounds of papers that you feel are meaningless, then you may be in tears too.

Homework and You

Every time you give a homework assignment you are involving three groups of people in the homework process: your students, the parents and yourself. For homework to be effective, you must conscientiously give appropriate assignments, parents must provide support and motivation at home, and students must do the work themselves and to the best of their ability.

When you think about it, homework asks for a lot from everyone involved. And you are the key. Homework starts and ends with you.

You are responsible for laying the groundwork for effective homework by:

- Teaching students how to set up a homework time, how to find a quiet place to work, how to do the work themselves, how to do their best work, and how to bring completed assignments back to school.
- Teaching parents when and how to help their children, how to reinforce good work and how to deal with children who will not complete homework.
- Assigning work that your students can do, giving clear directions, collecting and checking assignments and providing consistent positive reinforcement to both students and parents.

Yes, this is going to take time and effort on your part. But if you give homework, it is going to take your (and parents' and students') time and effort one way or another. *Homework Without Tears for Teachers* will help you make the time and effort spent as profitable as possible by giving everyone involved the skills they need.

Homework and Parents

If there is a common cry among educators, it is a plea for more parental support. While homework has the potential of eliciting that support from parents, many times its misuse does exactly the opposite. Too often the parents' only first-hand experience with their children's education is a nightly confrontation over homework.

Homework can be, however, a golden opportunity to positively involve parents in the education of their children. One thing researchers do agree on is the importance of parents' interest and involvement to children's success in school. The more parents provide positive support, the better their children will achieve.

Homework is a daily opportunity for parents to help their children do better in school. *Homework Without Tears* will show you how to give parents the directions they need to be an important, positive part of their child's education.

Homework and Students in Grades 4-6

Students in grades 4-6 may have difficulty with homework because they were not introduced to proper study skills in earlier grades. It is essential that you not assume that your students know how to select a study area, how to schedule homework time or even know how to take home assignments and bring completed homework back to school.   Even if you believe your students already have these skills, the lessons in Chapter 3, "How to Teach Your Students to Do Homework Responsibly," will provide a solid base for homework assignments throughout the year.

You may also encounter students who for one reason or another simply refuse to do their homework. Chapter 6, "What to Do If Students Do Not Complete Homework," will give you techniques to get them back on the homework track.

What is *Homework Without Tears*?

Homework Without Tears for Teachers is a systematic approach to effective homework based both on research and on the experience of master teachers. *Homework Without Tears for Teachers* will give you the ideas, materials and skills you need for yourself, your students and their parents to ensure homework is done consistently and responsibly.

This book will show you:

How to establish a homework policy.

- Guidelines for developing an effective homework policy and for communicating that policy to students and parents.

How to teach your students to do homework.

- Eight lesson plans to teach students to do homework responsibly.
- Parent Tip Sheets to involve parents in each lesson.

How to assign effective homework.

- Guidelines for determining effective homework assignments.
- Teacher-tested tips for collecting and correcting homework.

How to motivate students to do their homework.

- How to motivate individual students to do homework.
- Motivational techniques for your entire class.

What to do when students do not complete homework.

- Techniques you can use at school when students do not complete homework.
- Resource sheets for parents to use when their children do not do homework.

How to assign more creative homework.

- Creative Homework Models that can be applied to all subject areas.

Homework Without Tears for Teachers will make the homework process a more rewarding experience for you, your students and their parents. But the first step must be yours and there's no better time to start than right now.

Chapter 2
ESTABLISHING A HOMEWORK POLICY

Teachers who have an effective approach to homework start by developing a homework policy. The policy establishes a firm foundation for homework by stating your expectations for everyone involved in the homework process.

Your homework policy is important because it clearly spells out the type and amount of homework you will give, the manner in which you expect students to do their homework and the type and degree of support you expect from parents.

Many schools or districts already have a homework policy in place for you to use. If there is no such policy, it is important that you establish one on your own or with the help of your fellow teachers and your administrator.

A homework policy should:

Give a rationale for homework.

You cannot assume that students or parents understand why homework is given or how important it is. Therefore, you should explain the benefits of homework and why you are going to give it. For instance, your rationale could include that homework is important because:

1. It reinforces skills and material learned in class.
2. It prepares students for upcoming class topics.
3. It teaches students to work independently.
4. It aids in evaluating student progress.

Explain the types of homework you will assign.

It is important that both parents and students know that you are doing your part to ensure that students have the ability to do the homework you assign.

Your policy should state that homework you assign will require only those skills students have already learned in class.

Chapter 4, "5 Steps to Giving Effective Homework Assignments," will cover in detail the guidelines for assigning effective homework.

Inform parents of the amount and frequency of homework.

Research has shown that regular homework assignments produce more learning than less consistently assigned homework. It is important, therefore, for you to include in your homework policy:

1. The days of the week on which you will assign homework.
2. The amount of time it should take students to complete homework.

The amount of homework you assign will depend on your community, your district, your principal, your class and even the individual student. Research has shown that 45 to 90 minutes of homework per night is a workable time range geared toward the average student in grades 4-6.

Of course, these are simply guidelines. The length of assignments *must always be determined by the individual needs and capabilities of the students involved.*

Provide guidelines for when and how students are to complete homework.

For students to meet your expectations about completing homework, you must clearly define how you expect students to go about doing their assignments. Typical expectations include that:

- All assignments will be completed.
- Students will do homework on their own and to the best of their ability.
- Students will turn in work that is neatly done.
- Students will turn in homework on time.
- Students are responsible for making up homework assignments missed due to absence.

State that you will keep a record of assignments completed and not completed.

Your policy should state that you will keep a daily record of all homework assignments completed and not completed. The fact that you will check all homework is enough to motivate many students to do their homework. Also, this type of record keeping says something to both students and parents about the value you place on each and every assignment.

Explain how homework will affect students' grades.

Students and parents need to know if homework will be graded separately or as a percentage of another grade. Many schools list homework as a separate item on report cards. Others consider homework as part of a citizenship grade or a subject grade. Whatever system you or your school uses should be stated in your homework policy.

Let parents know how you will positively reinforce students who complete homework.

Research has shown that positive reinforcement is useful in motivating students to do homework. Your policy, therefore, should include:

- Positive rewards for individual students: praise, awards, notes home to the parents.
- Positive rewards that can be earned by the entire class.

Chapter 5, "How To Motivate Students to Do Their Homework," will explain in detail how to use positive reinforcement to motivate students to do their homework.

Explain what you will do when students do not complete homework.

If students choose to do their homework, they will enjoy the rewards you have described to them. If they choose not to do their assignments, they choose to accept the consequences of that choice, such as the loss of certain privileges.

It is important to note here that in some instances students may be prevented from doing homework by circumstances outside of their control. You must be sensitive to your own students and their home situations. Students should not lose privileges for not completing homework when it is not their fault.

However, for most students it is not that they *can't* do their homework, it is that they *won't* do it. Simply saying that you expect homework to be completed every night is not enough. It is with these students who choose not to complete their assignments that you must back up your words with action. (See Chapter 6, "What to Do If Students Do Not Complete Homework.")

When students choose not to do their homework, you can take action such as:

- Have parents sign completed homework every night.
- Have students miss recess to complete homework.
- Have students complete homework in after-school detention.
- Lower students' grades.

Homework missed for legitimate reasons must be explained in a signed note from the parents.

Clarify what is expected of the parent.

Research consistently shows that parents are a key factor in children's achievement in school. It follows, therefore, that parents must play an important role in the homework process. Since you do not follow the homework and the students home, it is up to parents to see that homework is completed. Your homework policy needs to cover the specific type of support you expect from parents. You should expect parents to:

- Establish homework as a top priority for their children.
- Make sure that their children do homework in a quiet environment.
- Establish a Daily Homework Time.
- Provide positive support when homework is completed.
- Not allow their children to get out of doing homework.
- Contact you if children have problems with homework.

While parents may agree in principal with all of these points, they may not know exactly how to go about providing the support you expect.

To help you gain the parental support you need, in Chapter 6 you will be given resource sheets to give to parents. These sheets give parents step-by-step instructions for what they must do to help solve the specific problem their child is having with homework.

How to Use the Homework Policy

If you have developed your own homework policy, give a copy to your administrator for approval. Some administrators may require that they have a copy of your homework policy on file. In any case, it is a good idea to share your policy with your administrator in case parents contact him or her with questions or problems. Your efforts can't be supported unless your administrator knows what your policy is.

Discuss the homework policy with students.

At the beginning of the school year or whenever you begin the *Homework Without Tears* program, present your homework policy to your students and have a discussion regarding the guidelines. Make sure that you allow enough time to answer all of the students' questions.

Send the homework policy home to parents.

Send a copy of your homework policy home to parents. It is important that all parents understand exactly what you expect of them and their children in the homework process. Send a letter home with the policy instructing the parents to discuss the policy with their children. Provide a tear-off section on the accompanying letter for both parents and students to sign acknowledging that they have read and discussed the homework policy. Then have the students bring the signed portion of the letter back to you.

Sample Homework Policy

Take a moment to go over the sample homework policy on the following page.

SAMPLE HOMEWORK POLICY

Dear Parent,

I believe homework is important because it is a valuable aid in helping students make the most of their experience in school. I give homework because it is useful in reinforcing what has been learned in class, preparing students for upcoming lessons, extending and generalizing concepts, teaching responsibility and helping students develop positive study habits.

I will assign homework Monday through Thursday nights. Homework should take students no more than one hour to complete each night, not including studying for tests and long-range projects. Spelling tests will be given each Friday. I will give students at least one week's notice to study for all tests, and one written report will be assigned each grading period.

I expect students to do their best job on their homework. I expect homework to be neat, not sloppy. I expect students to do the work on their own and only ask for help after they have given it their best effort.

I will check all homework. I strongly believe in the value positive support plays in motivating children to develop good study habits. I will give students praise and other incentives when they do their homework.

If students choose not to do their homework, I will ask that parents begin checking and signing completed homework each night. If students still choose not to complete their homework, they also choose to lose certain privileges. If students choose to make up homework the next day, their homework will be accepted but they will receive a one-grade reduction on that assignment. If they choose not to make up missed assignments, students will receive a fifteen-minute detention for each homework assignment missed. The first time a student receives a detention for missed homework, I will contact the parents.

If there is a legitimate reason why a student is not able to finish homework, the parent must send a note to me on the day the homework is due stating the reason it was not completed. The note must be signed by the parent.

I feel that parents are the key to making homework a positive experience for their children. Therefore, I ask that parents make homework a top priority, provide necessary supplies and a quiet homework environment, set a daily homework time, provide praise and support, not let children avoid homework and contact me if they notice a problem.

Parents should help their children with homework if a problem arises, but only after children have tried their best to solve it on their own. In no case, however, should parents do homework for their children.

I will be sending home lessons to help students learn how to do homework. I ask that students and parents go over these lessons together.

Teacher's Signature

Chapter 3
HOW TO TEACH YOUR STUDENTS TO DO HOMEWORK RESPONSIBLY

Many students have difficulty with homework simply because they lack proper study habits. They forget to bring assignments back to class, they study in front of the television set or while talking on the phone, and they always seem to have time in their busy schedules for everything but homework.

This chapter gives you a series of lessons that will teach your students—and their parents—how to do homework responsibly. The assignments contained in the lessons are designed to be the first homework assignments the students receive during the school year. If possible, the lessons should be presented in the first week or two of school. What the student learns from these lessons can then be applied to homework assignments the rest of the year.

To be most effective, these lessons must be presented before any academic homework is assigned.

The Following Lessons Are Included In This Chapter:

Lesson 1: Introducing the Homework Policy

Lesson 2: Returning Homework to School on Time

Lesson 3: Setting Up a Study Area

Lesson 4: Creating a Homework Survival Kit

Lesson 5: Scheduling Daily Homework Time

Lesson 6: Doing Homework on Your Own

Lesson 7: Rewarding Yourself for Homework Success

Lesson 8: How to Schedule Long-Range Projects

Each lesson includes the following components:

A **Teacher's Lesson Plan** outlining the rationale, objective and procedure for the lesson. The lesson plans are contained within this chapter.

A **Student Worksheet** to reinforce and expand the lesson. Student Worksheet reproducible masters are in the Appendix section of this book.

A **Parent Tip Sheet** designed to keep parents informed of specific ways they can help their children do homework successfully. Reproducible masters are in the Appendix. (Note: There is no Parent Tip Sheet for Lesson 1.)

To use the lessons in this chapter most effectively, first determine a time frame in which you will teach the lessons.

Note: All the lessons need to be taught together in the space of one or two weeks.

Follow this sequence when presenting each lesson:

- Read the lesson plan to familiarize yourself with the rationale, objectives and activities for the lesson.
- Make one copy for each student of the Student Worksheet(s) and Parent Tip Sheet for the lesson.
- Teach the lesson to your students:
  - Introduce the concept.
  - Discuss the concept with your students.
  - Explain the homework assignment and distribute Student Worksheets.
  - Distribute and discuss Parent Tip Sheets. Have students take home their worksheets and Parent Tip Sheets.
- Follow up as indicated on the lesson plan.

You are now ready to begin teaching your students to do their homework responsibly. Proceed to Lesson 1 on the next page.

Lesson 1
INTRODUCING THE HOMEWORK POLICY

RATIONALE —————— A homework policy establishes a firm foundation for homework by stating the expectations and responsibilities of everyone involved in the homework process—teacher, students, and parents. In Lesson 1, students will be introduced to your homework policy and learn exactly what is expected of them regarding homework.

OBJECTIVE —————— After being introduced to the homework policy in class, the students will take home a copy of the policy, discuss it with their parents, obtain appropriate signatures, and return signatures to school.

MATERIALS —————— Homework Policy, Letter to parents

PROCEDURE —————— **INTRODUCE THE IMPORTANCE OF EVERYONE—TEACHER, PARENT, AND STUDENT—BEING INVOLVED IN HOMEWORK**

1 Tell students that homework involves more than just the student. Explain that homework is a responsibility that involves the teacher, the students, and their parents.

2 Ask students to tell what they think their own homework responsibilities might be. List their ideas on the board.

Examples:

- Remembering to take homework assignments home.
- Remembering to do the assignment.
- Remembering to bring homework back to school.
- Doing the work neatly.
- Trying to do the homework on your own.

3 Explain to students that during the next few days you will be teaching them some special skills that will help them do their homework assignments more responsibly.

4 Now ask students to talk about what their parents' homework responsibilities might be. List their ideas on the board.

Examples:

- Making sure the student has a place to study at home.
- Reminding the student to do homework.
- Making sure that necessary homework supplies are available.
- Helping the student get to the library when necessary.
- Reading and checking rough drafts.

5 Tell students that it is important for parents, too, to learn about better ways of doing homework—and what they can do to help their children. Explain that during the next few days you will be sending Parent Tip Sheets home that will give their parents lots of information about helping with homework.

DISCUSS HOW A HOMEWORK POLICY WILL HELP EVERYONE—TEACHER, STUDENT AND PARENTS—UNDERSTAND AND FULFILL THEIR RESPONSIBILITIES

1 Tell students that tonight you are going to give each of them a written homework policy to take home. Explain that a homework policy is a list of standards that will help students and parents understand their homework responsibilities. Read the policy standards to the class.

2 Explain why a homework policy is needed. (So that parents and students alike will clearly understand your expectations about homework.)

3 Tell about the positives you will use when homework is done appropriately. Explain the consequences that will be imposed when homework is not done.

4 Check for student understanding by having them paraphrase each of the standards you read.

5 Give each student a signed (by you) copy of the homework policy and a cover letter to take home to parents.

EXPLAIN THE HOMEWORK ASSIGNMENT: TAKE THE HOMEWORK POLICY HOME, READ IT WITH PARENTS, AND RETURN THE SIGNATURE PORTION TO SCHOOL

1 Explain to students that they are to read the homework policy with their parents that night. Tell them that after reading the policy together, you want the students *and* their parents to sign the accompanying letter in the appropriate spaces. (Show the signature portion of the letter.) Explain that their signatures will let you know that parents and students understand what is expected of everyone regarding homework.

2 Tell students that you want them to return the signed tear-off portion of the letter to school the next day.

FOLLOW UP

1 NEXT DAY Collect signed papers. Review the homework policy once more to make certain that all students understand their responsibilities.

2 Put up a charted version of the homework policy in the classroom.

3 Do your part in enforcing the homework policy by always following through with your positives and consequences. Be consistent. Let your students know that in your class homework is important.

Dear Parent,

I believe homework is important because it is a valuable aid in helping students make the most of their experience in school. I give homework because it is useful in reinforcing what has been learned in class, preparing students for upcoming lessons, extending and generalizing concepts, teaching responsibility and helping students develop positive study habits.

I will assign homework Monday through Thursday nights. Homework should take students no more than one hour to complete each night, not including studying for tests and long-range projects. Spelling tests will be given each Friday. I will give students at least one week's notice to study for all tests, and one written report will be assigned each grading period.

I expect students to do their best job on their homework. I expect homework to be neat, not sloppy. I expect students to do the work on their own and only ask for help after they have given it their best effort.

I will check all homework. I strongly believe in the value positive support plays in motivating children to develop good study habits. I will give students praise and other incentives when they do their homework.

If students choose not to do their homework, I will ask that parents begin checking and signing completed homework each night. If students still choose not to complete their homework, they also choose to lose certain privileges. If students choose to make up homework the next day, their homework will be accepted but they will receive a one-grade reduction on that assignment. If they choose not to make up missed assignments, students will receive a fifteen-minute detention for each homework assignment missed. The first time a student receives a detention for missed homework, I will contact the parents.

If there is a legitimate reason why a student is not able to finish homework, the parent must send a note to me on the day the homework is due stating the reason it was not completed. The note must be signed by the parent.

I feel that parents are the key to making homework a positive experience for their children. Therefore, I ask that parents make homework a top priority, provide necessary supplies and a quiet homework environment, set a daily homework time, provide praise and support, not let children avoid homework and contact me if they notice a problem.

Parents should help their children with homework if a problem arises, but only after children have tried their best to solve it on their own. In no case, however, should parents do homework for their children.

I will be sending home lessons to help students learn how to do homework. I ask that students and parents go over these lessons together.

Teacher's Signature

Lesson 2
RETURNING HOMEWORK TO SCHOOL ON TIME

RATIONALE ——————— Remembering to bring homework assignments back to school when they are due is an important responsibility a student must develop. Lesson 2 provides students with skills that will help them develop the habit of returning homework to school on time.

OBJECTIVE ——————— Students will choose a spot at home where they will put completed homework assignments each night. They will mark this spot with a "Homework Drop Spot" sign. Consistent use of this Homework Drop Spot will help develop the habit of always putting finished homework in the same place each night—thus making it easier to remember to bring it back to school.

MATERIALS ——————— Student Worksheet 2 (Appendix page 81),
Parent Tip Sheet 2 (Appendix page 93)

PROCEDURE ———————
INTRODUCE THE CONCEPT OF REMEMBERING TO BRING HOMEWORK BACK TO SCHOOL EACH DAY

1 Ask students to think about times they have forgotten to bring homework assignments back to school. Have them give reasons why they forgot (e.g., couldn't find it, were too rushed to remember, lost it).

2 Ask what happens at home on mornings when they can't find their homework. How do they feel? How do their parents feel? How do students feel back in class when they've done the homework assignment and left it at home?

3 Have students brainstorm ideas that might help them remember to bring homework assignments back to school each day.

DISCUSS WAYS OF HELPING STUDENTS REMEMBER TO BRING HOMEWORK BACK TO SCHOOL

1 Tell students that you want to introduce a new idea that will help them bring homework back to school on time.

2 Discuss with students the importance of getting themselves in the habit of putting their completed homework in the same place each night. (Explain that a habit is something that you do so often or for so long that you do it without thinking.) Ask students to share their ideas for special Homework Drop Spots where homework goes as soon as it is completed (Example: Assignment first goes into a notebook, then into a backpack, then in a spot by the front door).

3 Point out to students that if they consistently put homework in the same place each night it will soon become a habit.

EXPLAIN THE HOMEWORK ASSIGNMENT (WORKSHEET 2)

1 Tell students that you are giving them an assignment that will help them remember to bring their homework back to school. Explain that their homework that night will be to complete a Homework Drop Spot word search and to select a Homework Drop Spot at home.

2 Show Worksheet 2: Homework Drop Spot Word Search. Tell students that the words HOMEWORK, DROP, SPOT, and HABIT each appear many times in the word search. Students are to find and circle these words.

3 Tell students that they are to tape the completed word search to the Homework Drop Spot they have chosen at home. Encourage them to use this sign to remind themselves to always put their completed homework in the same place each night. Remind them that consistent use of the Homework Drop Spot will help them develop the habit of always putting homework assignments where they can find them the next morning.

SHOW PARENT TIP SHEET 2

1 Encourage students to compare and talk about what's happening in the cartoons.

2 Explain that the Parent Tip Sheet will give their parents information about helping the students choose a Homework Drop Spot at home.

3 Read the Parent Tips to them as appropriate.

4 Make sure students take the Parent Tip Sheet home.

FOLLOW UP

1 Ask a few students each day to share how their Homework Drop Spots are working so they can evaluate whether they need to make any changes, and so others can hear what works and what doesn't work.

2 Remember that the goal of this activity is to form a habit that the students will benefit from for the rest of the year. Be consistent in rewarding students when they bring homework assignments back on time.

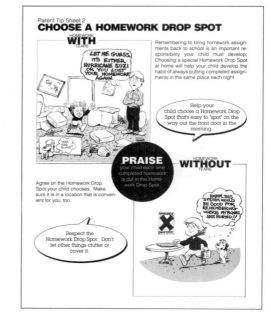

Lesson 3
SETTING UP A STUDY AREA

RATIONALE ——————————— Students—and their parents—must understand that to do homework successfully, they must have a place in which to work. The study area must be well-lit, quiet, and have all necessary supplies at hand. Lesson 3 will give students the skills and motivation they need to set up a proper study area at home.

OBJECTIVE ——————————— With the help of their parents, students will choose an appropriate study area at home. They will then draw a picture of their personal study area.

MATERIALS ——————————— Student Worksheet 3a (Appendix page 82), Student Worksheet 3b (Appendix page 83), "Do Not Disturb" sign (Appendix page 84), Parent Tip Sheet 3 (Appendix page 94)

PROCEDURE ———————————
INTRODUCE THE CONCEPT OF DOING HOMEWORK IN A STUDY AREA

1 Have individual students talk about where at home they have done homework assignments in the past. Was this a good place to do homework? What did they like about the location? What, if any, were some of the problems they had working in this location?

2 Share ideas about the following questions:

Should they do homework in a noisy room? Why or why not?

Should they do homework in front of a TV? Why or why not?

Should they do homework while they are eating? Why or why not?

Should they do homework outside while they are playing? Why or why not?

3 Ask students to brainstorm what a proper study area should be. Make sure that the following points are included: An appropriate study area is one that is well-lit, quiet, and has all necessary supplies at hand.

DISCUSS SETTING UP A PERSONAL STUDY AREA AT HOME

1 Encourage students to share ideas for study area locations in their homes. Ask these students to tell why the location would be a good place for doing homework.

2 Make it clear to students that even if they usually do most of their homework after school in another location (such as the library or an afterschool care program), they still need a place at home where they can study at other times.

3 Emphasize that a study area can be in any part of the home: kitchen, bedroom, living room, den, etc. It doesn't matter where it is as long as it's a place where the student can concentrate and get his or her work done.

4 Discuss the importance of making a personal study area FUN as well as FUNCTIONAL.

- Talk about setting up a study area in such a way that you want to use it— that it suits the way you study.

- Have the students list on the board all the things they think belong in a study area. Divide the list into two categories:

FUNCTIONAL—Study Area Basics

(the necessities)

Examples:
- Desk or table
- Chair
- Lamp
- Wastebasket
- Supplies (see Lesson 4 on "Creating a Homework Survival Kit")

FUN—Study Area Extras

(the personal touches)

Examples:
- Desk mat of colored poster board
- Comfortable, decorative pillows
- Small plant or vase of flowers
- Doodle pad
- Posters or signs
- Favorite photographs

Note: Recognize that some of your students may have real difficulty finding a quiet place to study at home. They may live in an overcrowded apartment, the environment may be unstable or chaotic, their parents may be unresponsive to their study needs, etc. Help these students explore study area alternatives. Talk about what they can do to help themselves by taking action on their own.

SOME SUGGESTIONS:

1 Find another place to do homework, such as the library or a friend's house.

2 Consistently ask their parents to support their study efforts by keeping sisters and brothers quiet during homework time.

3 Ask parents if one room can be off limits to others in the family during homework time.

4 Arrange with a brother or sister to do homework at the same time.

Be sure to ask students to give suggestions of their own to this problem.

EXPLAIN THE HOMEWORK ASSIGNMENT (WORKSHEETS 3a and 3b)

1 Tell students that, with their parent's help, they are to choose a study area at home. Explain that the homework assignment that night will be to draw a picture of the study area they have chosen.

2 Show Worksheet 3a: My Study Area. Tell students to draw a picture of the study area they have choosen. Point out that the lower part of the worksheet contains spaces for students to write information about their study area. In addition, there is a

Name _____
Date _____

My Study Area

In the space below, draw a picture of the study area you have chosen at home. Then complete the lower part of this worksheet.

My study area will be in _____
This will be a good location for studying because _____

I will do my homework in this study area.
Student signature _____
I have agreed upon this study area for my child.
Parent signature _____

space for a parent's signature, and a space for the student's signature. Emphasize that these signatures mean that both parent and student have agreed upon this study area, and that the student agrees to do homework in this location. Instruct students to return the worksheet to school with both signatures.

3 Show Worksheet 3b: Study Area Poster. Encourage students to cut out, color and use this poster to "personalize" their study area. If time allows, let the class brainstorm their own homework phrases and slogans.

SHOW PARENT TIP SHEET 3

1 Encourage students to compare and talk about what's happening in the cartoons.

2 Explain that the Parent Tip Sheet will give their parents information about helping students set up their own study areas.

3 Read the Parent Tips to them as appropriate.

4 Make sure that students take the Parent Tip Sheet home.

FOLLOW UP

1 NEXT DAY Collect Worksheet 3a. Display the returned study area pictures on a classroom bulletin board.

2 Have students color the "Do Not Disturb" sign (Appendix page 84). Tell them to hang it in their study area at home.

3 As a related art project, have the students decorate cans or jars to be used as special pencil or pen holders at home. They can also cover various shaped boxes to be used as desktop organizers.

Lesson 4
CREATING A HOMEWORK SURVIVAL KIT

RATIONALE _____ To complete homework assignments effectively, students must have available at home a collection of basic materials. A Homework Survival Kit—containing the materials needed to do homework—will help students get their homework done appropriately, and on time. Lesson 4 will give students the skills they need to create a Homework Survival Kit.

OBJECTIVE _____ Students will complete a Hidden Pictures puzzle by identifying items that are needed for doing homework. They will apply the information learned in this activity to the creation of their own real Homework Survival Kits.

MATERIALS _____ Student Worksheet 4 (Appendix page 85),
Parent Tip Sheet 4 (Appendix page 95)

PROCEDURE _____ ### INTRODUCE THE CONCEPT OF CREATING A HOMEWORK SURVIVAL KIT

1 Tell students that an important part of getting homework assignments done at night is having all the supplies they need in their study area.

2 Ask students to talk about what happens at home when they can't find something they need in order to complete an assignment. (Example: A report is due the next day and they don't have a folder to put it in.) Share experiences of when *not* having the proper supplies really created a big problem for them or their parents.

3 Tell students that one way to solve this problem is by creating their own Homework Survival Kits. Explain that a Homework Survival Kit is a collection of all the materials they would need to do their homework.

DISCUSS THE KINDS OF MATERIALS THAT SHOULD GO INTO A HOMEWORK SURVIVAL KIT AND DIFFERENT WAYS TO KEEP THESE MATERIALS ORGANIZED

1 Have the students list on the board some of the kinds of materials that should go in a Homework Survival Kit. For each item listed, have students tell how it would help in getting different kinds of homework done.

2 Talk about some of the different ways students can keep all Homework Survival Kit materials in one place at home. Let the students brainstorm types of containers (boxes, drawers, etc.) that could be used.

3 Have samples of some containers available so that students can evaluate the pros and cons of different sizes, shapes, etc. (Is it big enough to hold everything? Is it so deep that things will get lost in the bottom?)

SUGGESTED MATERIALS FOR A HOMEWORK SURVIVAL KIT

pencils • markers • colored pencils • crayons
pencil sharpener • erasers • glue or paste • tape
writing paper • construction paper • stapler • hole punch
scissors • paper clips • ruler • dictionary • index cards
assignment book • folders for reports

EXPLAIN THE HOMEWORK ASSIGNMENT (WORKSHEET 4)

1 Tell the students that you are giving them an assignment that will help them remember what items belong in a Homework Survival Kit.

2 Show Worksheet 4: Homework Survival Kit Hidden Pictures Safari. Tell students that they are to find and circle all of the 19 Homework Survival kit items that are hidden in the picture. As each item is found, they are to list it on the back of the worksheet.

3 Explain to students that they are to have a parent sign the finished worksheet and are to return it to school the next day. Tell students that their parent's signature on this worksheet means that the parent agrees to help the student put together his or her own real Homework Survival Kit.

4 Emphasize to students that their parents are not expected to run out and buy everything on the list. Explain that a complete Homework Survival Kit is a goal, something to complete over time.

5 Remind students to put their completed homework assignments in the Homework Drop Spot!

Note: If some of your students do not have the means to obtain materials for a Homework Survival Kit, you can help by allowing them to take "portable" Survival Kits home from school. Let students take home specific materials they will need to complete a homework assignment (paper, markers, a pen, etc.). Have them carry these materials back and forth from home as needed. You might also check into the availability of supplies from school that could be given to students for the intent of helping with homework.

Keep in mind also that Homework Survival Kit items make excellent classroom rewards.

SHOW PARENT TIP SHEET 4

1 Encourage students to compare and talk about what's happening in the cartoons.

2 Explain that the Parent Tip Sheet will give their parents information about helping the students create their own Homework Survival Kits at home.

3 Read the Parent Tips to them as appropriate.

4 Make sure students take home the Parent Tip Sheet.

FOLLOW UP

1 NEXT DAY Collect the signed Hidden Pictures worksheets, check them off, and then return them to the students. Tell them to use the list on the back to keep track of what items they already have at home, and those that they need to add as they begin to create their own Homework Survival Kits. Tell students to check off each item as soon as they put it in their Homework Survival Kit.

2 Encourage students to share the names of local stores where they have been able to find the various materials for their Homework Survival Kits.

3 As a related art project, have the students decorate a small box that they can take home to use in their Homework Survival Kit to keep paper clips, crayons, pencils, etc.

Lesson 5
SCHEDULING DAILY HOMEWORK TIME

RATIONALE ———————
Homework—like other activities and responsibilities—must be scheduled into a student's life. Lesson 5 will teach students how to schedule Daily Homework Time that is compatible with personal and family activities, and that also reflects their own best learning styles.

OBJECTIVE ———————
Students will record their daily after-school activities to determine a time each day for homework. They will apply the information learned in this activity to scheduling Daily Homework Time .

MATERIALS ———————
Student Worksheet 5 (Appendix page 86),
Parent Tip Sheet 5 (Appendix page 96)

PROCEDURE ———————
INTRODUCE THE CONCEPT OF SCHEDULING DAILY HOMEWORK TIME

1 Ask students to talk about some of the problems they have had in getting homework done on time. Do they wait until late at night when they are too tired to do a good job? Do their parents "nag" them to get to work? Do other activities and responsibilities (sports, music lessons, babysitting, chores, etc.) ever interfere? Are students usually able to fit these other activities into their schedule? Why do they think that they are able to get to a ballgame (for example) on time, and yet homework is often hastily done at the last minute? The ballgame is scheduled!

2 Tell students that it's important to schedule a Daily Homework Time. Explain that Daily Homework Time is a pre-planned time set aside each day during which they will do their homework. Point out that the purpose of Daily Homework Time is to schedule homework into a student's life, just as other activities are scheduled.

Note: Be aware of the particular needs of your students. Some students have no structure—or scheduled activites (other than school)—at all in their lives. Emphasize to these students that just as knowing when school starts helps them get to class on time, Daily Homework Time will help them get homework done on time.

3 Ask students to talk about how Daily Homework Time might help them get homework done.

4 Tell students that there are two things to consider when setting up Daily Homework Time: (1) the external time patterns of already scheduled after-school activities and responsibilities (music lessons, sports practice, babysitting, chores etc.) and (2) their internal time patterns that help them know what time of day they function best for doing homework (e.g., right after school vs after a play break).

5 Ask students to name some of the activities that are part of their external time schedules. Do they usually get to these activities on time? Why do they think this is so? Reiterate that these activities are taken care of on time because they are usually scheduled. Homework must also become a scheduled activity.

DISCUSS PERSONAL TIME PATTERNS

1 Clarify the concept of personal time patterns by doing the following activity in class:

a. Read the Personal Time Statement below:

I do homework best:
- right when I get home.
- after a snack.
- after dinner.

b. Tell students to go to the left side of the room if the first part of the statement applies to them.

c. Tell students to go to the middle of the room if the second part of the statement applies to them .

d. Tell students to go to the right side of the room if the third part applies to them.

e. After all students have moved to one of the three areas, ask volunteers in each area to explain why that choice reflects their personal time pattern for the given statement.

2 Ask students why they think it's important to take into consideration their personal time patterns when deciding on the best time to do their homework.

EXPLAIN THE HOMEWORK ASSIGNMENT
(Worksheet 5)

1 Tell students that you are giving them an assignment that will help them schedule Daily Homework Time for one week.

2 Show Worksheet 5: Schedule Your Daily Homework Time. Explain to students that they are to fill in all of their scheduled after-school activities and responsibilities in the spaces shown. Point out that by filling in all scheduled activities for a given week, they can clearly see what time is available for homework. Emphasize that students should also think about their personal time patterns. If, for example, Monday afternoon at 4 PM and Monday night at 7 PM are both available for Daily Homework Time, the student should carefully consider which time is best for him or her. Tell students to determine a Daily Homework Time for each day of the week and write it in the spaces shown.

SHOW PARENT TIP SHEET 5

1 Encourage students to compare and talk about what's happening in the cartoons.
2 Explain that the Parent Tip Sheet will give their parents information about helping the students schedule Daily Homework Time.
3 Read the Parent Tips to them as appropriate.
4 Make sure students take home the Parent Tip Sheet.

FOLLOW UP

1 NEXT DAY Check to see that students have completed their Daily Schedules. Tell them to keep these schedules close at hand, either in their notebook, taped up in their study area, or in some other prominent location such as on the refrigerator. Encourage students to stick to these Daily Homework Times for a week.
2 ONE WEEK LATER Ask students to evaluate Daily Homework Time. How many followed their schedules?   Did it make a difference?
3 THROUGHOUT THE YEAR Make copies of the Daily Schedule (Student Worksheet 5) available for student use.

Lesson 6
DOING HOMEWORK ON YOUR OWN

RATIONALE —————— Doing homework independently teaches a student responsibility and builds confidence and self-esteem. In Lesson 6 students will be encouraged to take pride in doing homework assignments on their own.

OBJECTIVE —————— Students will use "positive message" acronyms (e.g. , W.O.W. —Wonderfully Organized Work) to identify homework assignments they are proud of having done on their own.

MATERIALS —————— Student Worksheet 6 (Appendix page 87),
Parent Tip Sheet 6 (Appendix page 97)

PROCEDURE —————— **INTRODUCE THE CONCEPT OF DOING HOMEWORK ON YOUR OWN**

1 Ask individual students to give examples of occasions when they did something on their own for the first time.
Examples:
- The first time a two-wheeled bike is ridden solo.
- The first time a student is paid for a job done outside the family.
- The first time a student cooks a meal on his or her own.

2 Talk about how they feel when they're able to do something all on their own that they previously needed lots of help doing.

3 Now ask students to share ideas about why it's important to do homework assignments on their own, without a parent's help. Stress the fact that although it may be *easier* to get work done if the student is always asking for—and getting—help, the student will not be learning. Point out that by doing homework on their own, and learning from the assignments, students will do better on classroom assignments, be able to contribute more to class discussions, and will be much more prepared for quizzes and tests. Also emphasize that by doing homework on their own they are learning to be responsible for themselves, and that's something to be very proud of.

DISCUSS WITH STUDENTS DIFFERENT WAYS FOR THEM TO DO MORE OF THEIR HOMEWORK ON THEIR OWN

1 Brainstorm ways for students to do more of their homework assignments on their own.
Examples:
- Call a friend if you need help in understanding or doing an assignment.
- Do the easiest parts of an assignment first so you feel successful. Tackle the hardest parts last.
- Ask for adult help only when you've tried it on your own and can't go any further.
- Give yourself positive messages about how proud you'll be when you get the work done. (Example: "I really am a terrific kid!")

EXPLAIN THE HOMEWORK ASSIGNMENT (WORKSHEET 6)

1 Tell students that you are giving them an assignment that will help them identify work they are proud of having done on their own.

2 Show Worksheet 6: W.O.W. Tell students that each of the squares on this worksheet contains an acronym that is a positive message about a homework assignment. Tell students that they will use the squares to identify homework assignments that they are particularly proud of having done on their own.

Be sure that students understand that an acronym is a word formed from the initial letters of other words. Here are some examples of well-known acronyms: M.A.D.D. Mothers Against Drunk Driving; N.O.W. National Organization of Women.

3 Read the acronyms on the worksheet to the students:

W.O.W. Wonderfully Organized Work

A.C.E. Assignment Creatively Executed

E.S.P. Extraordinarily Superb Project

4 Point out that there are two blank squares on the worksheet. Tell students that they are to invent a "positive message" acronym of their own for each of these spaces.

5 Tell students that they are to cut out the acronym squares and put them in their Homework Survival Kit. They are also to bring back one of the acronym squares that they have written.

6 Make sure that students understand that the rest of the squares are to be used whenever they wish to identify a homework assignment that they are proud of having done independently.

SHOW PARENT TIP SHEET 6

1 Encourage students to compare and talk about what's happening in the cartoons.

2 Read the Parent Tips to them as appropriate.

3 Make sure students take home the Parent Tip Sheet.

FOLLOW UP

1 Play *Acronym Grab Bag.*

a. Collect the acronym squares that students have written.

b. Put these squares into a box.

c. Ask students to one by one draw a square from the grab bag.

d. Have a student write the acronym on the board. The rest of the class tries to guess what the initials stand for.

2 Make sure to give students feedback when they have used one of the acronym squares to identify a homework assignment. Make your comments relate to the acronym. (Examples: "You really **ACED** this project." "**WOW!** Great work!")

3 After students have used up their acronym squares, have them mark papers with the acronym itself. Encourage them to keep using this self-reinforcing system throughout the year.

Lesson 7
REWARDING YOURSELF FOR HOMEWORK SUCCESS

RATIONALE —————————— Praise received from others is a powerful motivator. But students must also learn to take pride in their own efforts and to give themselves a personal "pat on the back" when they are pleased with their work. Lesson 7 teaches students the importance of rewarding oneself for a job well done.

OBJECTIVE ———————— Students will write a list of suggestions of ways that they can reward themselves for meeting their homework goals.

MATERIALS ———————— Student Worksheet 7 (Appendix page 88),
Parent Tip Sheet 7 (Appendix page 98)

PROCEDURE ———————— ## INTRODUCE THE CONCEPT OF REWARDING ONESELF FOR A JOB WELL DONE

1 Talk about the importance of giving yourself a pat on the back when you've done something you're proud of.

2 Ask students to tell of situations in which they've given themselves a reward for something they've done. Ask them how it felt.

3 Why is it a good idea to reward yourself?

DISCUSS WITH STUDENTS THE CONCEPT OF REWARDING THEMSELVES FOR DOING A GOOD JOB ON HOMEWORK

1 Tell students that it's also a good idea to reward yourself for doing a good job with homework. Ask them to tell about different times they might reward themselves:

Examples:

- When I bring homework back on time.
- When I do my homework on my own.
- When I keep my Homework Survival Kit filled.
- When I do my homework without being told to again and again.
- When I do very neat work.
- When I do an assignment very creatively.

2 Brainstorm ways students can reward themselves. Make sure the students understand that these must be rewards they have the power to give to themselves. Ask each student to suggest one reward that he or she would be able to give himself or herself.

Examples:

- Call a friend when homework is completed.
- Watch a special television show.
- Play a computer game.
- Fix a snack.
- Ride a bike or use a skateboard.
- Play with a friend.
- Have a special dessert.

EXPLAIN THE HOMEWORK ASSIGNMENT (WORKSHEET 7)

1 Tell students that you are giving them an assignment that will help them think about the different ways they can reward themselves for doing a good job.

2 Show Worksheet 7: A Treasure Chest of Rewards! Tell students that they are to "fill the treasure chest" with ideas for rewards they can give themselves. Emphasize once more that these rewards must be things that they really do have the power to give themselves.

SHOW PARENT TIP SHEET 7

1 Encourage students to compare and talk about what's happening in the two cartoons.

2 Read the Parent Tips to them as appropriate.

3 Make sure students take home the Parent Tip Sheet.

FOLLOW UP

1 NEXT DAY Collect and then return completed worksheets to students. Tell them to keep the sheet in their Homework Survival Kit as a reminder of ways to reward themselves when they've done a terrific job on homework!

2 As the year goes on, encourage students to share ways they've rewarded themselves for doing a good job with homework.

Lesson 8
HOW TO SCHEDULE LONG-RANGE PROJECTS

WHEN TO PRESENT THIS LESSON — At the time you give students any long-range assignment such as a written report, book report, or test study.

RATIONALE — Long-range assignments are often the most difficult assignments students are asked to do. This is primarily because students lack the time-management and organizational skills vital to completing the work. Lesson 8 teaches students how to schedule all the steps of a long-range project so that the deadline can be met.

OBJECTIVE — Whenever given a long-range assignment, the students will use the Long-Range Planner to break the assignment into a scheduled series of steps with a "mini-deadline" for each step.

Note: The *process* of learning to do a long-range project is as important to young students as the final project itself. Keep in mind that your goal is for students to succeed. By assigning mini-deadlines for each step of the project, you can more effectively intervene and keep students on track, on time, organized and effectively learning the process of handling a long-range assignment.

MATERIALS — Long-Range Planner (Appendix page 89), Parent Tip Sheet 8 (Appendix page 99)

PROCEDURE — **INTRODUCE THE CONCEPT OF BREAKING A BIG ASSIGNMENT DOWN INTO A SERIES OF LITTLE STEPS**

1 Tell students that they are going to be working on a long-range project. (Describe the specific project: written report, book report, test study, etc.)

2 Have students think back to the last assignment they had of this type. Ask how many students remember feeling overwhelmed by the project or felt a last-minute panic just before it was due.

3 Encourage students to talk about why they might have had these feelings.

Examples:

- They didn't plan ahead.

- They waited until the last minute to begin work.

- All the research books were checked out of the library by the time they finally got started.

- There was so much to do they just didn't know where to begin.

4 Tell students that you are going to teach them to plan and organize their project so that they will learn to avoid these problems. Tell them that the key to solving the problems is to break the big assignment down into a lot of little assignments, each with its own deadline.

DISCUSS THE LONG-RANGE ASSIGNMENT THAT YOUR STUDENTS WILL BE DOING

1 Describe the assignment in detail and give its due date.

2 Ask students to think about all the steps they have to do to get this assignment done. List ideas on the board. (Examples for a term paper: do research, check out books, write an outline, take notes, etc.)

3 Point out that, unless they organize all of these steps, it's very easy to get caught at the deadline without work being completed. For that reason, you and they are going to set up a series of mini-deadlines that will help them get the work done on time.

4 Write on the board the steps you have determined are required to complete all parts of this assignment. (Your steps will most likely encompass all of the suggestions given by the students.) Do not write the steps in their proper sequence.

Note: The examples below show a hypothetical series of steps for 3 different long-range projects. These steps may or may not meet the particular requirements of your assignment, and are used only as an example. Determine the sequence of steps you want your students to follow for the long-range project before presenting this lesson.

Examples of Steps for a Written Report

Step 1: Pick out a topic for the report.

Step 2: Do research.

Step 3: Decide what questions you want to answer in the report.

Step 4: Take notes about the topic.

Step 5: Write the rough draft.

Step 6: Write the final draft.

Examples of Steps for a Book Report

Step 1: Choose a book.

Step 2: Read the book; Take notes as you read.

Step 3: Write a rough draft of the book report.

Step 4: Write a final draft of the report.

Examples of Steps for Studying for a Test

Step 1: Organize all test material.

Step 2: Make test study cards.

Step 3: Answer study questions at the end of the chapter.

Step 4: Review all material.

5 As a whole-class activity, have the students sequence these steps in their logical, proper order. Which step would come first? Second? etc. Ask students to explain their reasons for the order. After the class is in agreement, have one student write the final sequenced list on the board.

EXPLAIN HOW TO USE THE LONG-RANGE PLANNER

1 Hold up a copy of the Long-Range Planner. Tell students that using a Long-Range Planner before they do anything else on the assignment will help them schedule their big, overwhelming project into smaller, more manageable steps. Explain that each of the steps listed on the board will have its own deadline. If they meet all these deadlines, then the final deadline should be no problem!

2 Distribute a copy of the Long-Range Planner to each student.

a. Instruct the students to copy the steps for doing the long-range project from the board. Show them where to write the steps on the Long-Range Planner.

b. Tell students to fill in the final due date on the "Date to Be Completed" space of the last step they filled in.

3 Say to students, "Now let's come up with deadlines for each of the other steps. How long do you think it will take you to complete Step 1?" Share ideas and agree upon a deadline for the first step. Continue in this manner until deadlines have been set for each of the steps. Work back and readjust deadlines as needed, so that everything will be done by the final deadline.

4 Finish the lesson by emphasizing the importance of sticking to these mini-deadlines. Tell the students that you will be checking their progress at each deadline.

5 Tell students to take the Long-Range Planner home that night and go over it with their parents. Point out that next to each "Date to Be Completed" space on the Planner there is a space for a parent's signature. Tell students that you will expect their parents to sign as each mini-deadline is met. The parent's signature will verify that their child has completed the step.

SHOW PARENT TIP SHEET 8

1 Encourage students to compare and talk about what's happening in the cartoons.

2 Explain that the Parent Tip Sheet will give their parents information about how to use the Long-Range Planner.

3 Read the Parent Tips to them as appropriate.

FOLLOW UP

1 Post a schedule of the mini-deadlines in the classroom. Tell students that on these dates you will be checking their work-in-progress. Explain that on these dates you will expect to see their Long-Range Planner signed by parents, and the current status of work done on the project.

2 Follow through by checking students' work at each mini-deadline. Provide plenty of praise and positive reinforcement as students meet these deadlines.

3 Give each student a supply of Long-Range Planners to keep in his or her study area. Encourage them to use the Long-Range Planner for any project that involves many steps and a lengthy period of time in which to complete it.

Chapter 4
5 STEPS TO GIVING EFFECTIVE HOMEWORK ASSIGNMENTS

Chapter 3 of this book provides lessons to teach your students how to do homework responsibly. But that's only part of the picture. The ultimate quality of your homework program—and its benefit to your students—depends upon the *effectiveness* of the homework assignments you give.

> Homework is **not** effective when it is hastily assigned as students are walking out the door at the end of the day.

> Homework is **not** effective when it has no learning objective.

> Homework is **not** effective when it bears no connection to classroom lessons.

> Homework is **not** effective when students do not have the necessary skills to complete it independently.

Keep in mind that each time you give a homework assignment you are asking three groups of people—yourself, your students, and their parents— to invest their time and energy. It is, therefore, extremely important that your homework assignments warrant this investment—and that time is being used to its maximum advantage. Consider this: Students typically do one hour of homework a night, four nights a week. That's four hours of concentrated study—as much studying as occurs in any one classroom day. Homework has the potential to give you an additional day of learning each week— learning that can be enhanced by effective homework assignments.

What determines an effective homework assignment?

To be utilized as an effective educational tool, homework must be recognized as a *process*. The homework process begins when you first plan your classroom lesson. This is the time when you should focus on the objective of the homework assignment you intend to give. The process continues as you decide the *type* of assignment to give, as you create or choose that assignment, and as you introduce it to the class. The homework process doesn't end until the assignment has been collected, commented upon or graded and returned to the student.

Each step of this process is a vital component of an effective homework assignment.

To help guide you through the homework process, *Homework Without Tears for Teachers* provides the following 5 Steps to Giving Effective Homework Assignments:

Step 1: Determine the learning objective of the homework assignment you are going to give.

Step 2: Make sure the homework assignment you choose fits the homework learning objective.

Step 3: Introduce the assignment to students clearly and effectively.

Step 4: Follow a pre-determined plan for collecting homework efficiently and in a time-saving manner.

Step 5: Utilize a variety of "Homework Correcting Shortcuts" for correcting homework.

STEP 1: Determine the learning objective of your homework assignment.

Before you give any homework assignment, you must first know exactly *why* you are giving it. To ensure that homework is more than busywork, you must clearly determine your learning objectives. You must ask yourself, "Why am I giving this assignment?"

> Is your objective to have students **review and practice** specific skills or material learned in class?
>
> Is your objective to **prepare** your students for an upcoming class topic?
>
> Is your objective to have students **apply skills** or concepts learned in class to new situations?
>
> Is your objective to have students **integrate a variety of skills** into a long-term assignment?

When you take time to determine the objective of your assignment, you help ensure the quality of that assignment by:

1 Giving yourself the opportunity to make sure that the learning objective is really worth pursuing. Are students going to learn from this task, or will they be filling their time and heads with unimportant facts or details?

2 Making sure that the learning objective is appropriate for all students.

3 Choosing or designing the type of assignment that would best fulfill the learning objective.

Note: Get into the habit of giving as much thought to your homework assignments as you do to your classroom lessons. The best time to plan your homework is when you are planning the lesson. Look at the homework assignment as an extension and enhancement of a specific lesson. Record your homework assignments in your planbook right alongside the day's lesson. Take time to evaluate the flow of homework within one subject area. Is it leading somewhere, or is it simply a disorganized potpourri of tasks?

STEP 2: Make sure the homework assignment you choose fits the homework learning objective.

Your learning objective will determine the type of assignment you give. Homework assignments generally fall into four categories:

Practice Homework

Preparation Homework

Extension Homework

Long-term Homework

Practice Homework
Objective: To review and practice specific skills or materials covered in class.

Practice assignments are the most commonly given homework. Because practice assignments can be readily given through supplemental worksheets as well as textbooks, they can also be the most easily misused and *overused* type of homework. Don't fall into the trap of handing out practice worksheets or other drill work just to give out homework.

Keep in mind that your goal in giving a practice assignment must be to practice a *particular* skill that *has been covered in class*. Don't assign practice homework that is a conglomeration of lots of skills. For homework to be effective, the students must clearly be able to see what skill they are practicing.

Examples of practice homework assignments:

"Circle the pictures that have the long a sound."

"Answer the review questions at the end of Chapter 4."

"Write a synonym for each of the following words:"

"Do the even-numbered problems on page 33."

"Use each of this week's spelling words in a sentence."

When should you assign practice homework?

Ask yourself: Is my objective to have students review and reinforce specific skills or material they have learned in class? Do the students *need* to practice this skill? Have they already mastered this skill?

Guidelines for Assigning More Effective Practice Homework Assignments

- Don't give practice assignments if students do not need to practice that skill.

- Make sure that the practice assignment covers material covered in class.

- Assign practice homework only after you have determined that the student can do the work with reasonable success. Don't expect parents to "teach" skills to their children.

- Make sure a practice assignment focuses on a particular skill.

- Don't overdo drill assignments. Keep in mind that students who already grasp a concept don't need the practice, and would be better served and challenged by other types of homework. (Example: Why ask a student who already knows how to spell a word to write it ten times?) Likewise, students who don't understand a concept will just be reinforcing errors.

- Because it's sometimes difficult to be certain just who did a practice assignment (Mom, Dad, sister, brother, or the student), it's a good idea to occasionally follow such assignments with a quiz to determine if learning is taking place.

- Avoid the temptation to hand out "last-minute" practice worksheets just because you haven't planned anything else. Any homework is **not** better than no homework at all.

Additional Ideas for Improving the Effectiveness of Practice Homework

Assigning practice homework that matches your students' varied abilities *and* also raises their level of thinking need not require greater amounts of teacher preparation time. You can still give textbook assignments and utilize supplemental and workbook worksheets. However, *how* you use these materials is one of the keys to assigning more effective homework.

Here are some ways to use textbooks and workbooks creatively and at the appropriate level:

- Instead of assigning all students the same 30-problem page, have each student select 5 or 10 problems on the page that show what they are able to do.

- Set a time limit that each student is expected to spend on a homework assignment and accept the number of problems the student does in that time. Have a parent signature verify the time.

- Instead of assigning 30 problems on a page, have students do the top 3, middle 3, and bottom 3.

- Have students complete a few math problems in their text and then write more of their own on the same concept.

- Ask students to do 1 or 2 math story problems from the text, then make up 2 similar story problems based on situations from their own lives.

- Instead of *defining* spelling words, have students use the words in a poem or creative story.

- Ask students to make up 5 questions about a chapter in a textbook that they think would tell whether someone really understood the chapter. Exchange questions with other students.

- Have students select 12 words (for example) from a story they have read in their reading book. Give them specifics for choosing these words: words that describe how people feel; words that describe how things look; words that describe how things move, etc. Have students write the words in alphabetical order.

- After reading a story in the reader, ask students to write a different ending to the story.

Preparation Homework
Objective: To prepare students for an upcoming class topic.

Preparation homework is given when you want students to prepare on their own for an upcoming lesson. Properly assigned, preparation homework can serve to stimulate interest in the upcoming topic.

Examples of preparation homework:

"Read about the upcoming election in today's newspaper. List three issues that the candidates are discussing."

"Read pages 60-68 in your science book. Be prepared to describe the major processes in the water cycle."

"Watch the program *Earthquake* on channel 6 tonight. Be prepared to talk about one measure your family can take at home to prepare themselves for a large quake."

Note: Each of the preparation homework examples above asks the student to obtain specific information as an objective. Since the homework is covering new material, it is important that the student knows why he or she is doing this assignment.

When should you assign preparation homework?

Ask yourself: Is my goal to prepare students for an upcoming class topic? Will I follow up this assignment with related material in class?

Guidelines for Assigning More Effective Preparation Homework Assignments

- Make sure that your assignment is specific. Students must understand before they begin *why* they are doing this assignment.

- *Always* follow up a preparation homework assignment with a related lesson in class.

- Use a variety of materials for preparation homework assignments: newspaper, TV, magazines, interviews, etc.

Extension Homework
Objective: To apply concepts or skills learned in class to new situations.

The most meaningful and motivating learning occurs when students are asked to *apply* what they have learned in school to other situations. Homework, because it's done away from the classroom, provides the perfect opportunity for students to practice this transfer of learning. (A recognized goal of education is for students to be able to transfer learning from one context to another.) An extension homework assignment is one of the best uses you can make of homework.

Examples of extension homework:

"Measure your room at home. Find out the square footage."

"Interview an adult that you know. Ask him or her to talk about . . . ."

"Pretend that the main character in (the story we read today) came home with you for a day. What would you do? What would you talk about? What would the visit be like?"

"Sort the cans and boxes of food in your home into three categories. What are those categories? Why did you choose them?"

When should you assign extension homework?

Ask yourself: Is my goal to have students apply what they have learned in class to new situations?

Guidelines for Assigning More Effective Extension Homework Assignments

- Keep in mind that any subject matter is appropriate for extension homework.

- Brainstorm with students to come up with ways that they can apply what they've learned in school to other situations.

- Try to give extension homework as often as possible.

- See the Creative Homework Models (Chapter 7) for ideas for extension assignments. Start off with these lessons and you'll soon be coming up with lots more of your own!

Long-Range Homework
Objective : To integrate a variety of skills into a long-range project.

A long-range homework assignment requires the student to take many of the skills learned in class and build upon them to create something new. A long-range project requires the student to collect and organize information, turn that information into a different form, manage time, and enhance the project creatively. In short, a long-range assignment asks the student to "put it all together" to demonstrate a wide variety of skills.

Examples of long-range homework:

- Book report
- Term paper
- Science project

When should you assign long-range homework?

Ask yourself: Is my goal to give students an assignment that requires them to utilize a variety of skills (including time management and creativity)?

Guidelines for Assigning More Effective Long-Range Homework Assignments

- Keep in mind that in a long-range project, the *process* is even more important than the final result. With assignments such as book reports, term papers, etc., your learning goals must also include time management and organizational skills.
- Long-range projects can easily overwhelm a student. Help your students break down a long-range project into a series of more manageable steps. (See Lesson 8: How to Schedule Long-Range Projects, page 30.)
- Set a series of interim deadlines to keep students on track.
- Be consistent in checking these deadlines.
- Teach students the skills they need to fulfill all requirements for the project: note taking, writing an outline, research skills, etc.

Additional points to keep in mind when designing and choosing homework assignments:

The homework assignment must not require the student to do something he or she does not know how to do.

Before a homework assignment is given, you must determine that each student has the skills (and, perhaps, resources) necessary to do the work. Keep in mind that most homework assignments are expected to be done independently. It makes no sense to give a student an independent assignment that he or she lacks the skills to complete.

The assignment is not too much or too long.

Don't fall into the "more is better" trap. (This is particularly applicable to practice assignments.) Keep your objective for the assignment in mind. If, for example, 10 problems will let you know whether or not a student understands a specific math concept, why ask for 30? Remember: If a student grasps a concept he or she doesn't need the practice. If the student does *not* understand the concept, he or she will just be reinforcing errors.

The written directions are clear and concise.

Few things are as frustrating to students (and their parents) as incomprehensible directions. If directions to a fourth grader, for example, are meant to be read by that fourth grader, then make sure they are not written at a tenth grade level. Take time to re-read your directions.

Homework time will be spent on *learning*.

Don't waste student time on non-learning tasks. For example, don't ask students to copy questions, *then* write the answers. They are not learning anything while copying. Instead, have them answer the questions in a complete sentence that explains what is being asked. (Likewise writing spelling words ten times each.)

Homework should never be used as a disciplinary consequence.

Giving homework as a punishment is never appropriate. Remember that your homework goal is for learning to take place, and for the student to be a willing, capable participant in that learning. When you assign homework as a disciplinary consequence you confuse this goal with a negative factor, and only increase the likelihood that students will look upon homework with a less than enthusiastic response.

Keep in mind that the most effective homework program is one that consists of a variety of types of homework assignments. Just as your students at times need to review and practice skills learned in class, they also need to have the opportunity to extend those same skills and apply them to other situations, and to tackle more creative projects. When planning homework assignments, continue to ask yourself: "Will my students really learn appropriately from this assignment?" After all, if the student doesn't learn anything, there's no reason to give it.

STEP 3: Introduce the homework assignment clearly.

How you present your homework assignments to your students can be as important to the effectiveness of the assignment as the type of homework you assign. Research has shown that the way homework is presented affects the frequency with which students complete the homework and the motivation of students to do a good job on their homework assignments.

You can improve the effectiveness of your homework assignments—and increase your students' homework achievement— by following the simple guidelines below:

Always discuss the purpose of each assignment by saying, "Doing this homework will help you to (for example) correctly write plural possessives. . . ." (Preparing for this step will also help *you* make certain there is a clear objective for the assignment.)

Give clear, concise directions both orally and in written form. Don't write the assignment on the board without discussion or explanation. At the same time, don't expect students to remember directions that are only given orally. You can explain the assignment orally, but you should also write the directions on the board or on the top part of the homework worksheet, if applicable. Encourage students to rewrite directions on their assignment sheets in a way they will understand.

Write homework assignments in the same place each day. Designate a portion of the board as the "homework corner" and keep the assignments up all week so students who are absent can readily determine their make-up work.

Make sure you allow enough time for students to ask questions about the assignment. Don't wait until the last minute to give the homework assignment. Don't assume that students understand what is required of them just because they haven't asked many questions. To check on understanding, ask students to repeat the directions in their own words.

When appropriate, show samples of a successfully completed assignment to model what is expected or draw diagrams or pictures of what the final product should look like.

When appropriate, allow the students to start the homework assignment in class. If there is any confusion, the class can do a small part of the assignment together. You can help answer questions as they arise or ask students who understand the directions to model how they are doing the assignment.

When appropriate for the age and abilities of the students, give the class a list of homework assignments for the week. Let the students determine how to schedule their homework over the week, or you can designate due dates for some of the priority assignments. Allow students to turn in other assignments at the end of the week. In this way, you'll encourage students to learn how to manage their own time and allow them flexibility in scheduling other activities.

Communicate your homework policy to the class on a frequent basis. Remind the students how the policy will be enforced when assignments are incomplete or late. Be consistent with consequences and make-up procedures, especially at the start of the school year when patterns are being set and with students who are testing the limits of your homework policy.

Continue to emphasize to students the importance of homework. Reinforce this importance by collecting and correcting all or most of the homework assignments.

Try other "homework helper" ideas to further ensure student success with homework.

Institute a study hour after school.

This is particularly helpful for students who do not have a quiet place in which to study at home.

Assign a homework "study buddy" to each student.

Tell students to check with their study buddy when they are unsure of an assignment, or need to work through a problem with someone else. Make sure that study buddies exchange phone numbers!

Create a Homework Hotline for your class or school.

A Homework Hotline, staffed by teacher or community volunteers, gives each student the opportunity of having a supportive, helpful hand when they need it. This is especially beneficial for students who are on their own after school and are having specific problems with a homework assignment.

STEP 4: Use time-saving tips for collecting homework.

Finding efficient ways to collect students' homework assignments on a daily or weekly basis can save time and effort when it comes time to correct the homework. The suggestions that follow can be adapted to your own personal classroom style.

Have each student make a construction paper or manila file folder with his or her name on it. Each student should keep all completed homework in the folder at all times for daily, weekly or random checks. These personal homework folders can be stored in students' desks, or in a designated place in the classroom.

Make a different color-coded construction paper folder for each day of the week or each subject area. Make the students responsible for getting homework into the correct folders.

Make a dated folder for each day's (or each week's) homework assignments. Staple a copy of your class list inside each folder so you—or the students—can quickly check off or initial who's completed the homework on time. In this way, you can immediately reinforce those students who have met homework deadlines while following through on consequences for those with late or missed assignments, per your homework policy.

Clear off a countertop or book shelf and use masking tape labels to indicate which homework assignments go where. You can increase the likelihood of homework papers getting in the right place by using boxes (empty manila folder boxes are exactly the right size) to hold the assignments.

Assign a row or table monitor each week to collect homework.

Have homework handed in or collected the same time each day. Examples: When the late bell rings all homework should be on the desk ready to be collected; Before going to reading group, place homework in the appropriate folder.

STEP 5: Use "Homework Survival Shortcuts" for correcting homework.

Research indicates that it is vitally important that you collect all homework and either grade it or comment on it. Not every assignment must be *graded*, but the students must know that homework will be checked and commented upon in some way. Finding efficient ways to correct students' homework assignments can help you give students needed feedback on a consistent basis and, at the same time, can give you relief from "homework burnout."

Keep in mind that you can always shorten your correction time by balancing the types of assignments you give:

- Easy-to-correct assignments vs. hard-to-correct assignments.
- Assignments that students correct vs. those that you or an aide correct.
- Assignments that require grades vs. those that only need comments.
- Assignments with easy-to-check, definite answers vs. assignments that are more open to your commentary or opinion.

In addition to balancing the types of assignments you give, you can also shorten your correction time by utilizing some or all of the "Homework Survival Shortcuts" listed in this section.

Note: Because these shortcuts involve techniques like random checks and correcting only one aspect of a paper, they should be explained in advance to students and parents so that there is no misunderstanding over what you are doing.

Explain to students and parents:

All homework assignments *will* be collected and either graded or commented upon. On occasion, the comments may center on only one aspect of an assignment. On occasion (especially with practice assignments) you may do a random check of the work. Reiterate to parents that the goal of homework is for learning to take place and that your job as a teacher is to determine if that is happening. As a professional, you have many techniques at your disposal, and the knowledge of when to use them appropriately.

> **Once explained, these time-saving techniques will help make homework a more positive experience for everyone involved.**

Caution: These Homework Survival Shortcuts should be used only after appropriate homework "habits" have been developed (see Chapter 3, "Teaching Students to Do Homework Responsibly"). In addition, do not use these shortcuts when a brand new concept is being taught or early in the term.

Choose problems or questions at random to correct and grade or comment upon. Check off the others to indicate how many items were completed.

Select key problems or questions and only grade or comment upon those. Check off the others to indicate how many items were completed.

Select only one or two criteria to grade or comment upon. For example, instead of always checking for the correct answers on math homework, quickly scan each student's paper to see if they showed their computations and if they made their numerals neatly. Or, on written reports or stories, grade or comment on something new you taught the students about writing, such as using more active verbs or topic sentences with supporting details.

Give assignments that are appropriate for students to correct by themselves. Students may correct their own or another student's work. This technique saves you time and becomes a learning activity for the students.

The #1 Homework Correcting Rule

Whenever possible, comment in a positive way on how each student did on an assignment. Positive comments produce the best results! By commenting on the homework, you are letting students know that you place enough importance on their work to give it your time.

Summary

It is clear that the homework process requires a commitment from all involved. Assigning effective homework is your part of that commitment. When you take the time to ensure that the assignments you give are as effective as possible, you are ensuring in your classroom that homework means learning is taking place.

Chapter 5
HOW TO MOTIVATE STUDENTS TO DO THEIR HOMEWORK

Once you have taught students how to do homework and begin sending home assignments, you must provide motivation for students to complete homework on a regular basis.

For students who have had good school experiences and receive recognition at home, getting good grades may be motivation enough for them to do their homework. But the rest of your students may need something more to motivate them to complete homework. The most powerful motivational tool available to you is positive reinforcement.

Recognizing and rewarding appropriate behavior encourages students to continue that behavior. Students are more likely to continue to do homework when you give them praise for homework completed to your expectations. A simple "Thank you for turning your homework in on time" can go a long way toward encouraging students to continue their good work.

Positive reinforcement can also change behavior. When you have students who occasionally do not do their homework, give them extra attention or special privileges on days when they do complete their assignments. With students who only now and then miss homework assignments, it is important to first concentrate on positives when they choose to do their work. Many times these students are just looking for attention. Therefore, make sure they receive more attention when they do their assignments than when they don't do them.

Also, by praising students for doing a good job on homework, you make them feel better about their own abilities. And as you increase students' confidence and raise their self-image, you encourage them to do their assignments by themselves and to the best of their ability.

Keep in mind the following guidelines:

Positive reinforcement must be:

- Something the students like.
- Something you are comfortable using.
- Something used on a consistent basis.

Don't underestimate the power of positive reinforcement. Because of their home environment or previous experiences in school, many students lack and crave positive recognition. Your positive comments, notes and other incentives could be deciding factors in a student's self-confidence and success in school.

Positive Reinforcement You Can Give to Individual Students

Verbal praise

An effective form of reinforcement for doing homework is praise. Praise is appreciated by all children. It is particularly important for those students who are hard to motivate. Many children who do not do homework don't feel secure in their ability to succeed in anything relating to school. Keep in mind the enormous impact your praise can have on their self-esteem. With continual positive support, you can motivate students to develop a positive self-image and to approach homework with a confident, I-can-do-it attitude.

Use praise often and remember:

- Praise should be specific. For example, "John, your description of the storm in your story was terrific. I could almost feel the wind as I read it," rather than, "Good job, John."

- To be most effective, praise must be used consistently.

- Give positive comments on the content of homework rather than just its appearance.

- With older children, one-to-one praise is best so as not to embarrass the students in front of their peers.

Positive comments on completed homework

For many students, your continual praise is enough to stimulate and sustain enthusiasm about homework. But other children are more difficult to motivate with words alone. With these children, positive notes on their assignments can be very effective.

When you check homework:

- Add stickers, happy faces or other kinds of reinforcers for the students.

- Add positive, specific comments not just at the top of the homework paper, but throughout the assignment.

Oftentimes, a note of praise from you can be a much more powerful motivator than a good grade. Your notes can not only tell the students that you care about their *work* ("Jane, you put a lot of effort into this job. You really understood the lesson!"), but can also let students know that you care about *them* ("Seth, this is neatly done. I am proud of you!"). Remember, especially with hard-to-motivate students, building their self-esteem is key to helping them succeed.

Positive notes to parents

Students of all grade levels appreciate notes sent to their parents recognizing that they have done a good job on homework. (See Appendix pages 101 and 102 for Positive Notes for Parents.) Also, if parents are fulfilling their role in supporting homework, they too will appreciate knowing that their efforts are paying off. It is important that you make positive contact with parents on a regular basis. When using positive notes to parents:

- Set a goal to send home a certain number of notes per week.
- Be specific with your praise: "Sarah has been doing an excellent job following homework directions this week. You should be very proud."

Building a positive relationship with parents will also make it easier for you when you have to contact them about a problem. If you regularly send home positive notes, you communicate to the parents that you care about their children's success.

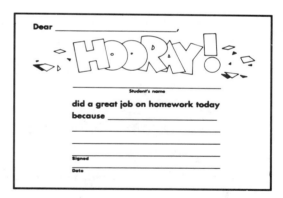

Homework cards

This method of reinforcement allows individual students to earn points toward a reward each time a homework assignment is completed.

- Place a card on each student's desk. The card is divided into ten or twenty boxes.
- Each day that homework is completed, place a check or a sticker in one of the boxes.
- When the entire card is filled, the student earns a reward such as extra free time, an award certificate, a night free of homework, etc.

Reinforcement Ideas You Can Use for the Entire Class

Here are a number of great ideas on how to set up positive reinforcement systems for your entire classroom. (Remember, the reward systems must be built around something the students like.) Below are examples of the types of systems teachers have found both fun and effective.

Bulletin boards to display student homework

By using a bulletin board featuring homework, you are giving the entire class a constant reminder of the importance you place on homework. Also, when you use the bulletin board to display homework that is done well, you are providing more positive reinforcement. All students enjoy seeing their good work posted for everyone to see. When using a homework bulletin board:

- Introduce how you are going to use the bulletin board when you present your homework policy to your students. (To display the best papers by row, etc.)

- Change the board weekly to allow as many students as possible to have their work displayed.

Homework chart

You can also set up a positive reinforcement system for the entire class by posting a homework chart on your bulletin board. The chart lists all of the students and provides a place to check every time a homework assignment is turned in on time. When the entire class (with the exception of those excused) turns in assignments on a given day, the class earns a point. When a certain number of points (5-10) are earned, the entire class gets a night free of homework or another privilege. This system is also effective because of the peer pressure it creates for all students to turn in homework on time. The guidelines for using a homework chart are:

- Every time all students turn in a completed homework assignment, one point is earned by the class.

- When a predetermined number points is reached, the class earns a reward such as extra free time, a popcorn party, extended recess, etc.

- Make sure that rewards can be earned in a relatively short period of time.

Using a homework chart also gives you an excellent means of documentation of homework completed and not completed. Also, since the chart covers several weeks, it allows you to spot patterns where students continually have trouble completing homework on a certain day.

Homework raffle

This reinforcement idea allows all students who complete their homework to have a chance at winning a raffle.

- The students are told to put their names on both the left- and right-hand upper corners of their homework assignment papers.
- When completed homework is turned in, you tear off all of the right-hand corners and put them into a jar or box.
- At the end of the week you draw a name or two from the jar. The students whose names are drawn win extra free time in class, a pass to miss a homework assignment, etc.

Summary

Positive reinforcement is one of the most effective tools at your disposal to ensure your students' success in school. Because it is so important, you should not leave your use of positives to chance. In addition to putting positive notes on students' homework, set a goal for yourself to send home at least two positive notes to parents per day.

These notes will not only motivate students to do homework, they will also build a positive relationship between you and the parents. One of the keys to effective homework is recognizing and encouraging the efforts of everyone involved in the homework process.

Chapter 6

WHAT TO DO IF STUDENTS DO NOT COMPLETE HOMEWORK

If you consistently use the motivational ideas in the previous chapter and still have students not completing their homework, you must take further action.

However, before using any of the techniques described in this chapter, you must first determine if there are circumstances beyond a student's control that are preventing him or her from completing homework.

Your record keeping will help you identify sudden changes in homework that could indicate a problem at home. Of course, your first source of information is the student. When presenting your homework policy to the students, avoid a harsh "no excuses, no extensions" attitude and encourage your students to come to you if they have a problem getting their homework done.

Some children may be embarrassed to tell you that they couldn't do their homework because they had to take care of younger brothers or sisters, or do the laundry, or make dinner. If you suspect a problem, you may want to talk with the parents, other teachers or the student's brother or sister to find out what the problem is.

The important thing to remember is not to arbitrarily take away privileges or lower grades when students do not complete their homework. Unfortunately, there are legitimate reasons why some students simply *cannot* complete their assignments at home. And if students feel they are being treated unjustly, they will soon begin to feel that nothing they do in school matters and resign themselves to failure. If you encounter students with problems such as this, listen to them and help them find solutions to the problem that is preventing them from doing homework.

If you determine it is the student who is at fault and is simply choosing not to complete homework, then you should consider using the techniques presented in this chapter.

This chapter presents two approaches you can use to get all students to complete their homework.

- In Part One, you will be given techniques you can use at school with the students.
- In Part Two, you are provided resource sheets to give to parents to help them solve seven of the most common homework problems.

Note: Any technique you use with students who do not complete homework must be clearly explained in your homework policy.

Before using any techniques for homework not completed, you need to ask yourself the following questions:

- Have you thoroughly explained homework assignments? Are the assignments appropriate to the student's grade level and have you determined that the student has the skills required to do the work successfully? (Review the guidelines in Chapter 4 on how to assign effective homework.)

- Are you sure that the student does not have a learning disability that is preventing him or her from completing homework?

- Are you sure that nothing has changed in the home environment to prevent the student from doing homework? (Has the student demonstrated ability in class to do the same level of work but is unable to do it at home?)

- Do you collect and check homework on a regular basis?

- Do you provide positive reinforcement on a regular basis?

If you have answered "yes" to all of these questions, and still have students who are not doing their homework, it is time for you to try the techniques suggested in this chapter.

PART ONE: WHAT YOU CAN DO AT SCHOOL WHEN STUDENTS DO NOT COMPLETE HOMEWORK

There are various techniques that are typically used by teachers with students who do not complete their homework assignments. We will give you examples of effective techniques, but you must choose those that you feel are appropriate for you and your students.

No matter what techniques you choose, you must have a means of keeping track of homework completed and not completed. Most teachers use their class record books to keep track of homework. It is important that you have these records available when contacting parents or enlisting the support of your administrator. You should also keep a record of notes sent home to parents and any disciplinary action (detention, etc.) taken with the student.

When determining the techniques you will use when students do not complete homework, keep in mind the techniques must:

- Be described in your homework policy.

- Be something you are comfortable using.

- Be such that they apply equally to all students.

Homework assignment books

The most effective way to make sure all students do their homework is to have them write their assignments in a homework assignment book (such as Lee Canter's *Homework Organizer*). Students keep the assignment book in their notebook, take it home each day and bring it back the next day. If appropriate, you may ask parents to sign the assignment book each night, indicating that homework assignments have been completed.

Using an assignment book prevents students from saying that they don't know what their assignments are and ensures that the parents know exactly what is expected of their children each night. Simply involving parents with an assignment book will solve many problems because the students know that their parents know what each night's assignments are.

Lowering grades on assignment

Many teachers use lowering grades on assignments or overall subject grades to motivate students. If you use this policy, remember that the objective is not to fail students, but to see that the homework gets done. If the students feel that they are already failing, there is little incentive for them to mend their ways and choose to do their homework. If lowering grades is not effective, contact the parents before giving students a failing grade.

The guidelines for using lower grades are as follows:

- The policy must be clearly explained to both students and parents before it is used.

- If students continue not to do homework, you must involve the parents.

- The policy must apply equally to all students.

Missed recess or lunch

A common technique is to have students make up missed homework during recess or lunch.

If you use loss of free time to make up homework, make sure that:

- Students finish their incomplete work by themselves.

- Talking is not allowed.

- No assistance is given from a teacher or supervisor. This is not helping time.

Note: If a student is always spending lunch or recess time doing homework, this may indicate a problem at home that is preventing him or her from working there. On the other hand, some students may prefer getting their work done at school. If you suspect this, it is time to involve the parents as suggested in the second half of this chapter.

Study hall or detention

Some schools set up homework study halls before school or after school that are manned on a rotating basis by teachers.

The guidelines for a Study Hall or Detention Room are:

- The room should be supervised by a teacher or other responsible adult.
- No talking; this is not a social hour.
- The students must work independently and only do homework.
- If the students disrupt, they must receive additional detention time.

The most important point to remember is that no matter what techniques you use, you must use them consistently. You must use the techniques every single time a non-excused homework assignment is missed. Your students must realize that every time they choose not to complete homework, they are choosing to accept the consequence of that action. It is only if you take action every single time that your students will believe that you mean business.

PART TWO: WHAT PARENTS CAN DO AT HOME TO SOLVE THE SEVEN MOST COMMON HOMEWORK PROBLEMS

If problems with homework persist no matter what you do at school, you need more involvement on the part of the parents. And you must involve the parents in a way that will provide you with effective support at home. All too many parents are at a loss for what to do at home to ensure that their children complete their homework assignments. It is important, therefore, that you supply the parents with the knowledge and skills they need to deal with their children. Remember, all parents want their children to succeed. The more you help parents, the more they will be able to help you and their children.

To help parents deal with their children effectively, *Homework Without Tears for Teachers* provides you with resource sheets to give to parents to help them solve each of the seven most common homework problems. These sheets give parents step-by-step solutions to most of the homework problems they will face. These resource sheets can be found in the Appendix on the pages listed below and tell parents what to do if:

For the parent(s) of _____

If your child will not do homework without your assistance, you must make sure that he or she is making a genuine effort in trying to work alone. If your child insists that you sit with him or her all night or continually begs for your assistance, follow the steps below.

Here's what to do when children will not do homework on their own:

1 State clearly that you expect your child to work alone.
Tell your child: "I expect you to do your homework without my help. I will not sit with you or do your work for you. I will not be available to answer questions every five minutes."

2 Provide praise and support when your child works on his or her own.
Monitor your child during Daily Homework Time. When you see your child working alone, say: "I am really proud of the way you are doing all of this work on your own. I knew you could do it!" Be consistent with your praise.

3 Help your child build confidence.
Many children will not work without your help because they feel their homework assignments are just too much to handle on their own. "Chunking" is a great technique to help your child gain the confidence needed to work on his or her own. "Chunking" means dividing a big assignment into smaller chunks you know can be handled successfully. For example, a 20-problem math assignment would be broken into 5 chunks of 4 problems each. The child is rewarded with a prize (raisins, peanuts, etc.) each time one of the chunks is completed until the assignment is finished.

4 Help your child only after he or she has genuinely tried to solve the problem on his or her own.
Be sure that your child has tried the problem at least twice before you agree to help. There will be times when something is really too hard for your child to understand, but be sure that you don't step in until he or she has made a genuine effort to solve the problem.

5 Provide additional incentives when appropriate.
Another technique to help children learn to work on their own is "Trade-Off." With this game, place a bowl of small candies, raisins or peanuts in front of your

Continued on back

child and say: "Each time you ask me for help with your homework, you will have to give me one of these candies (raisins, etc.). When they are all gone, I won't help you anymore. At the end of Daily Homework Time, you get to keep what's left."

6 Back up your words with action.
If the first five steps do not succeed in getting your child to work without your help, it is time to get tough. Make sure that your child knows that at the end of Daily Homework Time you will no longer be available to help and that your child will sit in his or her work space until the work is done—even if it means remaining there all evening. Be prepared for your child to use anger, tears or indifference to get you to back down. Let your child know that such tactics will not work and he or she will remain in the study area until he or she learns to work alone.

KEEP THIS IN MIND: Your child must learn to do homework on his or her own. Relying on you for help will only lead to greater dependence. Your child must develop the confidence to tackle any homework assignment on his or her own.

Before giving parents any of the resource sheets, make sure that you read them all thoroughly. While each sheet varies slightly, they all more or less give parents the following directions for solving their child's homework problem. (See next page.)

Parent resource sheets state that parents should:

1. Clearly and firmly state expectations to the child.
2. Institute Mandatory Homework Time (as explained on the resource sheets). Determine loss of privileges if child still chooses not to do homework.
3. Provide praise and support for work well done.
4. Provide additional incentives for continued good work.
5. Back up their words with action.
6. Contact the teacher if all else fails.

How To Use Parent Resource Sheets

- When there is a homework-related problem you need help with, contact the parents by phone or in a face-to-face meeting.
- With the parents, discuss the problem the child is having with homework, (i.e., takes all night to get it done, forgets to bring assignments home, etc.).
- Select the appropriate resource sheet and go over each of the steps to make sure the parents understand what is to be done. Then give or send the sheet home to the parents. Don't give the resource sheet to parents if you feel they will be intimidated by it. Just make sure they understand the steps they are to follow.
- Set a time (in a week or two) to follow up with the parents to determine whether the strategy has been effective or if further action is necessary.

Summary

When dealing with students who are having problems getting homework done, remember that the most powerful technique you can use is positive reinforcement. Give them extra praise and recognition when they do complete homework.

If extra positives don't solve the problem, first make sure that there are not circumstances beyond the student's control that are preventing him or her from doing homework. If there are not, use techniques such as the ones suggested in this chapter to let students know that not doing homework is unacceptable. And whatever technique you choose to use, you must use it consistently every time a homework assignment is missed.

Chapter 7
CREATIVE HOMEWORK MODELS

Most textbook and workbook assignments are designed at the practice and review level. However, the most meaningful and motivating learning occurs when students are asked to extend (apply) what they have learned in school to other situations in their lives. Homework, because it's done at home, provides the perfect opportunity for students to extend their learning.

The *Homework Without Tears for Teachers* Creative Homework Models supply a variety of formats for extension homework assignments in which *you* supply the content topic and the *students* apply what they have learned about that topic. The same Homework Model formats can be used over and over again for different subjects with different content specifics.

See the examples below and on the next page:

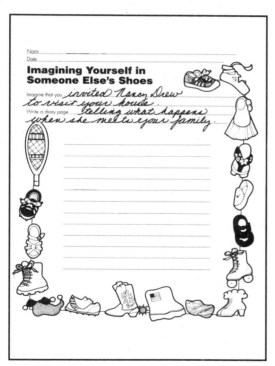

Sample Language Arts Application

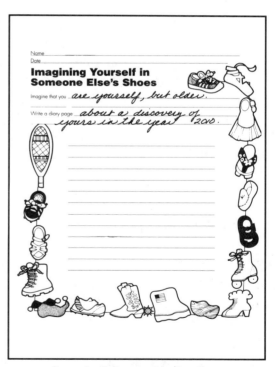

Sample Science Application

Sample Language Arts Application

Sample Social Studies Application

Each of the Creative Homework Models is designed at the extension (application) level to encourage students to really make learning relevant by seeing its application outside the classroom. As you examine the Homework Models, you will see that application of learning occurs when students *interview*, *imagine*, *make a model*, *take a side on an issue*, etc. The teacher's pages that follow describe each Homework Model format, show sample variations of use, and list many other suggestions for using the worksheets in different subject areas. The blackline reproducible pages are located in the Appendix, pages 119-126.

The Following Creative Homework Models Are Included In This Chapter:

Model 1: Interviewing for Information

Model 2: Sequencing

Model 3: Evaluating Different Opinions

Model 4: Imagining Yourself In Someone Else's Shoes

Model 5: Teach Your Parents Something That You Learned in School

Model 6: Using Found Objects to Make a Model of Something Learned

Creative Homework Model 1
INTERVIEWING FOR INFORMATION

This homework sheet is designed to motivate students to get information—facts, feelings, opinions, and personal stories—from others in the home environment about things being studied in school.

BEFORE YOU BEGIN
Make one copy of the Creative Homework Model 1 worksheet (Appendix page 121) for each student in the class. Pass them out.

EXPLAIN THE ASSIGNMENT TO STUDENTS
Tell them that they are going to interview someone at home about a specific topic being studied at school. Tell them the topic and have them write it on their worksheet in the appropriate spot. (See examples below.) When appropriate to the type of assignment, encourage students to use the 5W's: WHO, WHAT, WHEN, WHERE and WHY as one way to ask interview questions and also as a way to record the responses to their interview questions.

APPLICATION
This activity can be effectively used in different subject areas. You can probably think of many ways to use this homework sheet that will fit your specific curriculum needs and homework learning objectives. Here are some examples:

Language Arts
Interview someone at home to find out:
- their opinion of a movie or TV program you watched together.
- their opinion about a favorite book, short story, poem, or cartoon strip.
- their feelings about an exciting or emotional topic (for example: snakes, surprise birthday parties, embarassing moments, etc.).
- about their childhood.

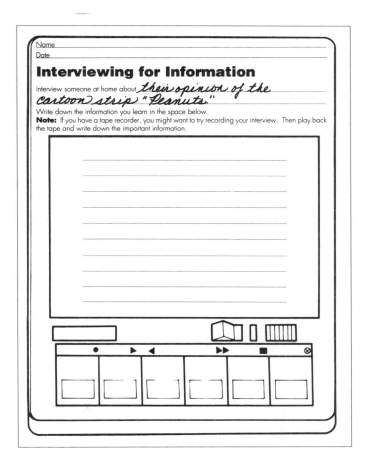

Science

Interview someone at home to find out:

- how simple machines around the house work.
- what to do in specific emergency situations (earthquake, tornado, fire, etc.).
- their feelings about a recent scientific break-through reported in the news.
- their opinion of the most time-saving invention of the last 5, 10 or 20 years.
- their opinion of a specific environmental issue.

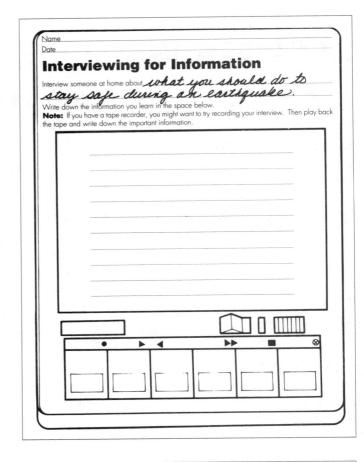

Social Studies

Interview someone at home to find out:

- about your family tree.
- more about your family's native country(ies).
- more about family traditions.
- about other countries someone in your family has visited.
- their opinion of something that is happening in another country.
- their opinion of an upcoming election.

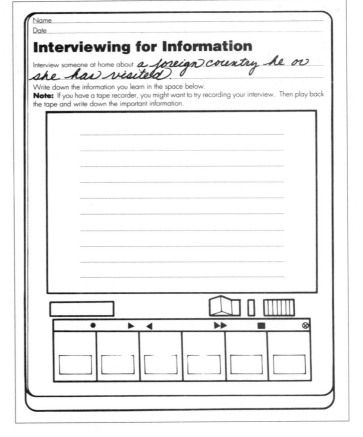

Creative Homework Model 2
SEQUENCING

This homework sheet is designed to encourage students to draw and/or write the steps in various sequenced activities they are learning about in school.

BEFORE YOU BEGIN

Make one copy of the Creative Homework Model 2 worksheet (Appendix page 122) for each student in the class. Pass them out.

EXPLAIN THE ASSIGNMENT TO STUDENTS

Talk about what it means to "draw or write steps" that show a specific activity. Give examples of the steps that might be followed for planning a party: 1. Pick a date. 2. Decide whom to invite. 3. Buy invitations. 4. Send invitations. 5. Plan food and activities. 6. Buy all supplies. 7. Get everything ready. 8. Have a party! Ask students to give examples of steps they follow when they do other activities (getting ready to do homework, setting the table, spending the night with a friend, etc.). Tell students that their homework assignment that night will be to write (or draw) the steps that show _____ (give specifics, including the number of steps you want the students to show). Have students write the instructions on their worksheet.

APPLICATION

This sequencing activity can be effectively used in different subject areas. You can probably think of many ways to use this homework sheet that will fit your specific curriculum needs and homework learning objectives. Here are some examples:

Language Arts

Draw or write the steps that show:

- what happened in a specific story.
- how to organize and write a letter.
- how to organize and write an outline.
- how to check a book out of the library.

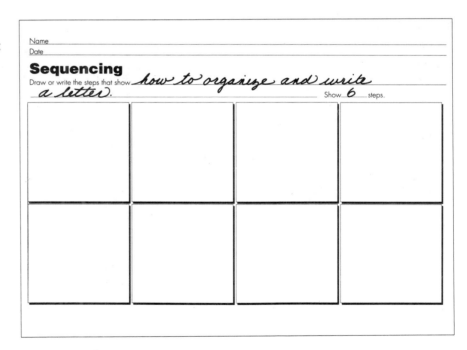

Science

Draw or write the steps that show:

- how we hear sound.
- photosynthesis.
- how blood is pumped through the body.
- how food is digested.
- how a fossil is formed.

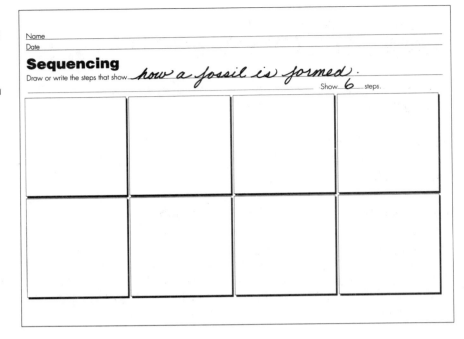

Social Studies

Draw or write the steps that show:

- how to make a salt and flour map.
- how a ship would travel today from San Francisco to China.
- how a ship would have traveled from San Francisco to China 200 years ago.
- the route of the Oregon Trail.
- how paper is produced.

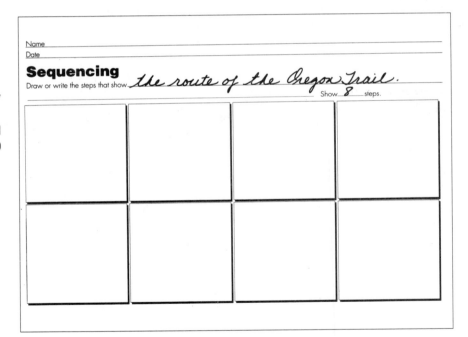

Creative Homework Model 3
EVALUATING DIFFERENT OPINIONS

This homework sheet is designed to help students think through the different sides of an issue or situation before forming their own opinion and stating their position.

BEFORE YOU BEGIN

Make a copy of the Creative Homework Model 3 worksheet (Appendix page 123) for each student in the class. Pass the worksheets out.

EXPLAIN THE ASSIGNMENT TO STUDENTS

Talk about the importance of recognizing that there is usually more than one side to any issue, from disagreements with friends to international politics. Explain that before forming an opinion on *any* issue, we must try first to examine that issue from all sides. As an introduction to the homework assignment, briefly discuss a current issue in your school or community about which there is a difference of opinion. Choose students to present all sides of the issue to the rest of the class. Give students their assignment (see examples below). Have them write it in the appropriate space on the worksheet.

APPLICATION

This activity can be effectively used in different subject areas. You can probably think of many ways to use this homework sheet that will fit your specific curriculum needs and homework learning objectives. Here are some examples:

Language Arts

List two reasons **for**, and two reasons **against**:

- children having their own telephones.
- children having their own television sets.
- children having to do chores around the house.
- children having pets.
- children going to year-round school.

Science/Health

List two reasons **for**, and two reasons **against**:

- sending human beings on space missions.
- having Daylight Saving Time.
- a local environmental issue.
- nuclear power plants.
- offshore oil drilling.
- mandatory seatbelt requirements.

Social Studies

List two reasons **for**, and two reasons **against**:

- a specific city issue.
- a specific national issue.
- a specific historical issue (example: the British tax on tea in 1773).

Creative Homework Model 4
IMAGINING YOURSELF IN SOMEONE ELSE'S SHOES

This homework sheet is designed to encourage students to put themselves in different roles—real and imaginary—based on characters from stories they read and on real-life heroes and heroines from their science and social studies readings.

BEFORE YOU BEGIN
Make a copy of the Creative Homework Model 4 worksheet (Appendix page 124) for each student in the class. Pass the worksheets out.

EXPLAIN THE ASSIGNMENT TO STUDENTS
Tell students that this assignment will give them the chance to "put themselves in someone else's shoes." Share ideas about what that means. Tell students the assignment and have them write it in the appropriate space on the worksheet. To start students off on the right foot, ask them to close their eyes for a couple of minutes and imagine that they are "in that person's shoes" right now. How does it feel? What are they thinking about? What do they look like? What does the world look like to them? Suggest that students try this technique at home when they begin to do their assignment.

APPLICATION
This activity can be effectively used in different subject areas. You can probably think of many ways to use this homework sheet that will fit your specific curriculum needs and homework learning objectives. Here are some examples:

Language Arts
Imagine that you:

- invite a character from a story you are reading to visit your house. Write a diary page telling what happens when he or she meets your family.

- could choose one of the characters from a story you are reading to be your best friend. Write a diary page telling how you would spend a day together.

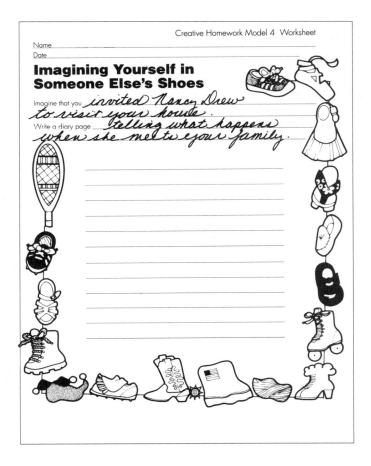

Science

Imagine that you:

- are (name a scientist you are studying). Write a diary page describing how you made one of your discoveries.
- are yourself, but older. Write a diary page about a discovery or invention of yours in the year 2010.
- are making an amazing scientific discovery. Write a diary page describing your invention.

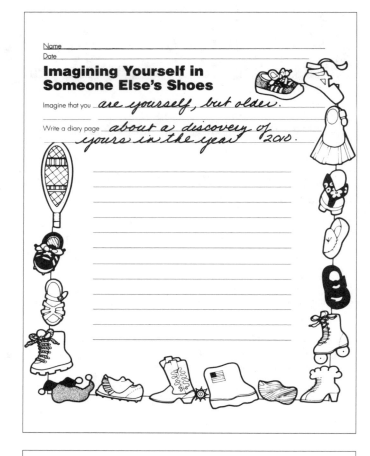

Name _____
Date _____

Imagining Yourself in Someone Else's Shoes

Imagine that you _are yourself, but older._

Write a diary page _about a discovery of yours in the year 2010._

Social Studies

Imagine that you:

- are (name a famous explorer or pioneer). Write a diary page telling about going to a new land.
- are (name a person currently being studied in class). Write a diary page about one of your achievements or adventures.
- are a child living in (name a time and place currently being studied in class). Write a diary page telling about a day in your life.
- are visiting (name a country or place currently being studied in class). Write a diary page telling about your trip.
- are a child who has time-traveled to the twentieth century from (name a time and place currently being studied in class). Write a diary page telling about your experiences.

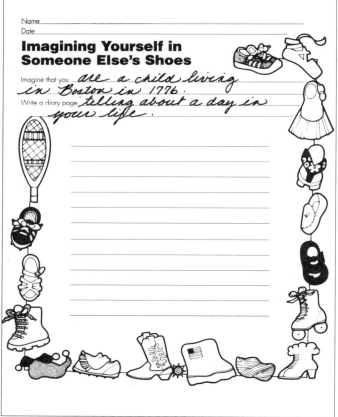

Name _____
Date _____

Imagining Yourself in Someone Else's Shoes

Imagine that you _are a child living in Boston in 1776._

Write a diary page _telling about a day in your life._

Creative Homework Model 5

TEACH YOUR PARENT SOMETHING THAT YOU LEARNED IN SCHOOL

This homework worksheet is designed to encourage a dialogue between child and parent about what's being learned in school, and to increase student learning by providing a different perspective from which to view a subject.

BEFORE YOU BEGIN
Make a copy of the Creative Homework Model 5 worksheet (Appendix page 125) for each student in the class. Pass the worksheets out.

EXPLAIN THE ASSIGNMENT TO STUDENTS
Tell students that this assignment will give them the opportunity to teach their parents something they have just learned in class. Explain that they are to go home and teach three facts about _____(give the specific assignment, making sure that the subject matter is something that they are working on in class).
1. Have them write the assignment in the appropriate space on the worksheet.
2. Ask students to look at Part One on the worksheet. Explain that they are to write the facts they are going to teach in these three spaces. (Each student can choose his or her own facts, or you can assign them.)
3. Point out that in Part Two they are to decide *how* they will teach these facts. Share ideas about ways that information can be taught (oral presentation, charts or diagrams, reading from a book). Talk about which methods students think would be most effective for teaching the facts.
4. In Part Three, students are to create test questions to give their parents after the lesson has been taught. Tell students to work out the questions on the front of the worksheet, then copy them on the back of the worksheet to give to their parents after the lesson has been taught.

APPLICATION
This activity can be effectively used in different subject areas. You can probably think of many ways to use this homework sheet that will fit your specific curriculum needs and homework learning objectives. Here are some examples:

Language Arts
Teach your parent three facts about:
- how to check a book out of the library.
- how to use the card catalog file.
- the Dewey Decimal System.
- how to use an encyclopedia.
- the parts of a book.
- organizing an outline.

Name _____
Date _____

Teach Your Parent Something That You Learned in School

Directions:
Teach your parent three facts about *the Dewey Decimal System*

Part One
Write the 3 three facts you are going to teach in the spaces below:

1 _____
2 _____
3 _____

Part Two
Plan how you are going to teach these three facts. Are you going to give an oral presentation, show charts or diagrams, read from a book. Will you ask your parent to take notes. In the space below, write how you will teach your lesson.
_____
_____

Part Three
Create three questions that will let you know whether or not your parent really learned the facts you taught. Use the spaces below to write your questions.

Question 1 _____

Question 2 _____

Question 3 _____

Copy these questions on the back of this worksheet. This will be your parent's test!

Part Four
Teach your lesson, then give your parent the test questions written on the back of this worksheet.

Science/Health

Teach your parent three facts about:

- how sound travels.
- latitude and longitude.
- photosynthesis.
- dental hygiene.
- bicycle safety.
- a specific scientist.
- a specific type of landform.

Name _____

Date _____

Teach Your Parent Something That You Learned in School

Directions:
Teach your parent three facts about *how sound travels*.

Part One
Write the 3 three facts you are going to teach in the spaces below:

1 _____

2 _____

3 _____

Part Two
Plan how you are going to teach these three facts. Are you going to give an oral presentation, show charts or diagrams, read from a book. Will you ask your parent to take notes. In the space below, write how you will teach your lesson.

_____

_____

Part Three
Create three questions that will let you know whether or not your parent really learned the facts you taught. Use the spaces below to write your questions.

Question 1 _____

_____

Question 2 _____

_____

Question 3 _____

_____

Copy these questions on the back of this worksheet. This will be your parent's test!

Part Four
Teach your lesson, then give your parent the test questions written on the back of this worksheet.

Social Studies

Teach your parent three facts about:

- the Oregon Trail.
- a specific geographical feature of the United States.
- the establishment of Jamestown (or another settlement).
- a specific historical figure.
- your state's history.
- your state's natural resources.
- pioneer life in America.

Name _____

Date _____

Teach Your Parent Something That You Learned in School

Directions:
Teach your parent three facts about *the Grand Canyon*.

Part One
Write the 3 three facts you are going to teach in the spaces below:

1 _____

2 _____

3 _____

Part Two
Plan how you are going to teach these three facts. Are you going to give an oral presentation, show charts or diagrams, read from a book. Will you ask your parent to take notes. In the space below, write how you will teach your lesson.

_____

_____

Part Three
Create three questions that will let you know whether or not your parent really learned the facts you taught. Use the spaces below to write your questions.

Question 1 _____

_____

Question 2 _____

_____

Question 3 _____

_____

Copy these questions on the back of this worksheet. This will be your parent's test!

Part Four
Teach your lesson, then give your parent the test questions written on the back of this worksheet.

Creative Homework Model 6

USING FOUND OBJECTS TO MAKE A MODEL OF SOMETHING LEARNED

This homework sheet is designed to encourage creativity by asking students to use simple objects they find at home to make models of things they've learned about in school.

BEFORE YOU BEGIN
Make one copy of the Creative Homework Model 6 worksheet (Appendix page 126) for each student in your class. Pass out the worksheets.

EXPLAIN THE ASSIGNMENT TO STUDENTS
Have students look at the "found objects" border on the worksheet. Explain that "found objects" are things that can be found around the yard or in a park (like sticks, leaves, or rocks), around the house (like clothespins, empty Kleenex boxes, toilet paper rolls, Popsicle sticks), or around the neighborhood (like aluminum cans, pieces of wood, Styrofoam food containers). Ask students to give examples of other objects that might be found in their environment. Explain that their homework assignment will be to make something (give the assignment) out of found objects. Have the students write the assignment in the appropriate space on the worksheet. Point out that the worksheet has spaces for students to write down information about their project. Read the instructions together.

APPLICATION
This "found object" activity can be effectively used in different subject areas. You can probably think of many ways to use this homework sheet that will fit your curriculum needs and homework learning objectives. (See examples that follow.) Note: Many of these assignments will require more than one night to complete. Work with students to establish deadlines. Check up on their progress at regular intervals. Because it's fun to do, this activity is a good introduction to long-range assignments for younger students.

Language Arts
Use found objects to make:

- something interesting to look at. Give it a name and write a story about it.
- a diorama of a scene from a story you are reading.
- a diorama of a scene from a story you are writing.
- something unusual to look at. Write a limerick about it.
- something beautiful to look at. Write a haiku about it.
- something funny to look at. Write as many adjectives as you can think of to describe it.

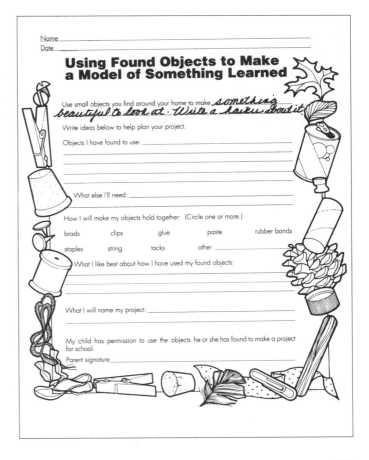

Science

Use found objects to make:

- something that moves forward.
- something that has a working lever.
- something that has a working pulley.
- a model of the layers of the earth.
- a model of the solar system.

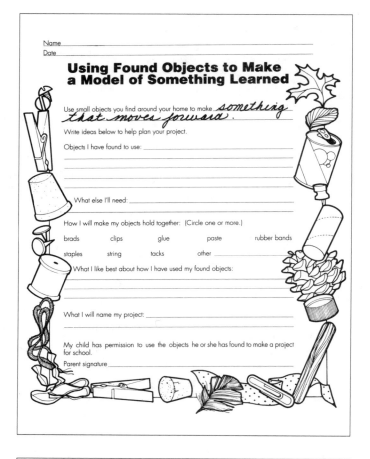

Social Studies

Note: This assignment is particularly appropriate to give when culminating a study unit in social studies.

Use found objects to make:

- a diorama of a town, city, or farm.
- a model of a kind of transportation.
- a model of a pioneer sod hut and farm.
- a relief map of a specific state or country.

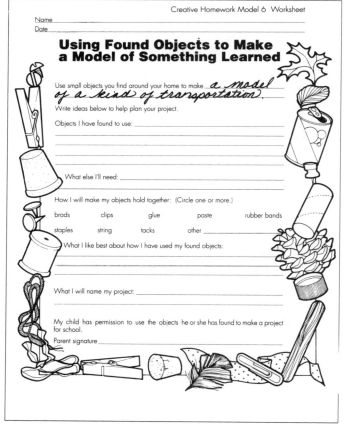

CONCLUSION

There is no doubt that homework can be a valuable part of the education process for all involved. It can help students develop the study skills they need to achieve better in school and develop a sense of responsibility. Homework can provide a way for parents to be productively involved in their child's education. And for you, the classroom teacher, homework can provide a valuable extension of the school day to reinforce your efforts in the classroom.

The key to making all of these benefits possible lies with you. All of the positive aspects of homework shrink to insignificance if the homework you assign is inappropriate for your students. The value of homework is relative. It is relative to the daily efforts you make to ensure that every homework assignment is meaningful and appropriate. But it is only with these efforts that you, your students and their parents can enjoy the rewards of homework completed responsibly, consistently. . . and without tears.

APPENDIX

STUDENT WORKSHEETS FOR HOMEWORK LESSONS

Pages 81-89 of the Appendix contain the reproducible Student Worksheets that correspond to the homework lessons provided in Chapter 3, "How to Teach Your Students to Do Homework Responsibly." Each of these worksheets has been designed to both reinforce the learning objective of the lesson, and to extend that learning into the home. Keep in mind that all of these homework lessons should be presented within a two-week time period. Therefore, it would be helpful to run off copies of all the worksheets (one per student of each worksheet) before you begin teaching the homework unit.

Student Worksheets:

Homework Without Tears for Teachers

Name _____

Date _____

Homework Drop Spot Word Search

Find and circle the words* HOMEWORK, DROP, SPOT, and HABIT in the word search below. The words may appear vertically, horizontally, forward, backward, or diagonally. Good luck!

```
H T I B A H A B I T R S Q V L N
B O R T W O M S H O M E W O R K
U C M I F M G G D R O P S P O T
K L N E O E U R T S H N A T H S
R D T W W L M C D P F H J A W
O R O I R O D W H I B O M Q B V
W O P B Z R R T M O L L T I I U
E P S A G K O K H L M S P O T H
M N D H I V P S A B H E R R Q A
O T T R B E E P B D R A W Z O B
H M M R O B G O A Z R I B O F I
J K A L U P J T T V M O N I R T
M Z U G G L T A R S S E P A T K
A H O M E W O R K D R O P H L A
I S P O T V T I B A H R T O P S
L R S P O R D K R O W E M O H I
```

Each word appears 7 times

X marks the Homework Drop Spot!

When you have completed the word search, tape this sheet to the Homework Drop Spot you have chosen. Use the sheet for at least one month to remind you to always put your completed homework in the same place each night.

Name _____

Date _____

My Study Area

In the space below, draw a picture of the study area you have chosen at home.   Then complete the lower part of this worksheet.

My study area will be in _____

This will be a good location for studying because _____

_____

I will do my homework in this study area.

Student signature _____

I have agreed upon this study area for my child.

Parent signature _____

Name _____

Date _____

Study Area Poster

Color the poster on this page.   Hang it up in your study area.

Homework Without Tears for Teachers   © Lee Canter & Associates Inc.

Name _____

Date _____

Homework Survival Kit
Hidden Picture Safari

Circle the 19 Homework Survival Kit items hidden in this picture. As you find each one, list it on the back of this worksheet. Check off each item on the list when you add the real one to your own Homework Survival Kit.

Homework Survival Kit items: pencils - markers - colored pencils - crayons - pencil sharpener - erasers - glue or paste - tape - writing paper - construction paper - stapler - hole punch - scissors - paper clips - ruler - dictionary - index cards - assignment book - folders for reports

I agree to help my child put together a Homework Survival Kit.
Parent signature _____

Name _____

Date _____

Schedule Your Daily Homework Time

Do this worksheet with a parent.

Write down all scheduled activities (music lessons, sports practices, etc.) and responsibilities (babysitting your brother or sister, doing chores, etc.) for each day of an average week so you can clearly see what time is available for homework. From the time available each day, think about your personal time patterns and write in the best time for you to do homework each day. Mark your selected Daily Homework Time for Monday, Tuesday, Wednesday, and Thursday in the spaces shown.

Daily Schedule

Monday

HOMEWORK TIME:

3:00 PM_____	7:00 PM_____	_____
4:00 PM_____	8:00 PM_____	to
5:00 PM_____	9:00 PM_____	_____
6:00 PM_____	10:00 PM_____	

Tuesday

HOMEWORK TIME:

3:00 PM_____	7:00 PM_____	_____
4:00 PM_____	8:00 PM_____	to
5:00 PM_____	9:00 PM_____	_____
6:00 PM_____	10:00 PM_____	

Wednesday

HOMEWORK TIME:

3:00 PM_____	7:00 PM_____	_____
4:00 PM_____	8:00 PM_____	to
5:00 PM_____	9:00 PM_____	_____
6:00 PM_____	10:00 PM_____	

Thursday

HOMEWORK TIME:

3:00 PM_____	7:00 PM_____	_____
4:00 PM_____	8:00 PM_____	to
5:00 PM_____	9:00 PM_____	_____
6:00 PM_____	10:00 PM_____	

Name _____

Date _____

W. O. W.

1. Read the acronyms on this page. Notice that each acronym is a positive message about homework.
2. Create a positive message (or more than one) of your own in the blank spaces.
3. Cut out the squares and put them in an envelope in your Homework Survival Kit.
4. Bring one of your own acronyms to school the next day for Acronym Grab Bag.
5. Use the cut-out squares to identify homework assignments that you are proud of having done on your own. Before you turn the assignment in, tape or staple an acronym square to the corner!

Name

Date

A Treasure Chest of Rewards!

Fill the treasure chest with ways you can reward *yourself* for meeting your homework goals. Remember, these rewards must be things that you really can give yourself.

 Homework Without Tears for Teachers

LONG-RANGE PLANNER

NAME_____ DATE _____

ASSIGNMENT_____ DUE DATE _____

STEP 1

_____

_____

Date to be completed _____

Parent's Initials_____

STEP 2

_____

_____

Date to be completed _____

Parent's Initials_____

STEP 3

_____

_____

Date to be completed _____

Parent's Initials_____

STEP 4

_____

_____

Date to be completed _____

Parent's Initials_____

STEP 5

_____

_____

Date to be completed _____

Parent's Initials_____

STEP 6

_____

_____

Date to be completed _____

Parent's Initials_____

STEP 7

_____

_____

Date to be completed _____

Parent's Initials_____

STEP 8

_____

_____

Date to be completed _____

Parent's Initials_____

PARENT TIP SHEETS FOR HOMEWORK LESSONS

Pages 93-99 of the Appendix contain the reproducible Parent Tip Sheets that correspond to the homework lessons provided in Chapter 3, "How to Teach Your Students to Do Homework Responsibly." Each of these Parent Tip Sheets has been designed to give parents the information they need to encourage their children to deal more successfully with homework. Keep in mind that all of the homework lessons should be presented within a two-week time period. Therefore, it would be helpful to run off copies of all the Parent Tip Sheets (one per student of each sheet) before you begin teaching the homework unit.

CHOOSE A HOMEWORK DROP SPOT

Remembering to bring homework assignments back to school is an important responsibility your child must develop. Choosing a special Homework Drop Spot at home will help your child develop the habit of always putting completed assignments in the same place each night.

Help your child choose a Homework Drop Spot that's easy to "spot" on the way out the front door in the morning.

PRAISE your child each time completed homework is put in the Homework Drop Spot.

Agree on the Homework Drop Spot your child chooses. Make sure it is in a location that is convenient for you, too.

Respect the Homework Drop Spot. Don't let other things clutter or cover it.

SET UP A STUDY AREA

To do homework successfully, your child must have a place in which to work. The study area must be well-lit, quiet, and have all necessary supplies.

Keep the radio and TV off while homework is being done.

Whenever possible, keep the study area off limits to brothers and sisters during homework time.

PRAISE your child when he or she does homework in the study area.

Help your child choose a location at home in which homework will be done. Even if your child does most homework at another location after school, there still should be a place in the home in which he or she can study.

Remember that your child does not need a lot of space to do homework. The kitchen table or a corner of the living room are fine, as long as they are well-lit and quiet during homework time.

CREATE A HOMEWORK SURVIVAL KIT

One of the keys to getting homework done is having supplies in one place. A Homework Survival Kit—containing supplies needed to do homework—will prevent your child from being continually distracted by the need to go searching for supplies, and will free you from last-minute trips to the store for folders, paper, tape, etc.

> If your child does homework at a location other than home (such as the library or an after-school care program) make sure that his or her homework supplies are available there.

> Respect your child's Homework Survival Kit. Don't use these supplies for other family needs.

AGREE with your child that it is his or her responsibility to remind you when any of the Homework Survival Kit materials are getting low and need replacing.

> Give Homework Survival Kit materials as gifts. A dictionary, for example, is a special present that a child will use over and over again.

These are the supplies needed for a Homework Survival Kit:
  *pencils ● *pens ● *writing paper ● colored pencils ● crayons ● markers ● ruler pencil sharpener ● erasers ● glue or paste tape ● construction paper ● hole punch stapler ● scissors ● paper clips assignment book ● folders for reports index cards ● dictionary

*These are the most important supplies your child needs. Try to obtain these items as soon as possible. Add additional homework supplies as you are able to.

You don't need to gather all the materials in one day, but don't wait too long. Your child needs these supplies to do his or her best job on homework.

SCHEDULE DAILY HOMEWORK TIME

HOMEWORK WITH TEARS

I'M SORRY DAD, BUT GROWING UP IS A FULL TIME JOB AND I JUST CAN'T FIT HOMEWORK INTO MY SCHEDULE.

Daily Homework Time is a pre-planned time set aside each day during which your child must do homework. During Daily Homework Time all other activities must stop; your child must go to his or her study area and get to work.

Tell your child that homework is to be done during a regularly scheduled Daily Homework Time.

Help your child determine the length of time needed each day for homework.

Have your child determine his or her scheduled after-school activities and responsibilities for the week and write them in the designated spaces on the Daily Schedule.

PRAISE your child when homework is completed during Daily Homework Time.

HOMEWORK WITHOUT TEARS

Encourage your child to identify his or her best personal time patterns for doing homework. (Example: right after school vs. right after dinner)

Tell your child to determine the best time period each day to be set aside for Daily Homework Time.

OH HI PAUL, LET ME SEE... I THINK I CAN PENCIL YOU IN AFTER HOMEWORK TOMORROW ABOUT 7PM... BUT PLEASE CALL TO CONFIRM...

LET'S SEE... ...SLEEP... ...EAT... ...CHASE CATS... ...SLEEP...

DAILY SCHEDULE

Have your child write the Daily Homework Times in the spaces shown on the Daily Schedule.

Check your child's completed Daily Schedule for accuracy. Make sure that the homework times chosen are appropriate.

Post the Daily Schedule in a prominent location. Encourage your child to stick to the schedule!

CHILDREN MUST WORK ON THEIR OWN

HOMEWORK **WITH** TEARS

> A "D" ON YOUR HOMEWORK!! AREN'T YOUR PARENTS GOING TO BE MAD?

> YOU BET! THEY WORKED ALL NIGHT ON THIS.!!

Homework teaches children responsibility. Through homework, children learn skills they must develop if they are to grow to be independent, motivated, and successful adults: how to follow directions, how to begin and complete a task, and how to manage time. By encouraging your child to work on his or her own, you are helping develop these important life skills.

> Check to see that your child is doing homework at the proper time.

PRAISE
your child when he or she does homework independently. Let your child know just how proud you really are!

HOMEWORK **WITHOUT** TEARS

> Suggest that your child call a friend if he or she needs help.

> Give your child help only if he or she makes a real effort to do the work first.

> NO, I DON'T NEED ANY HELP. REALLY MOM. DON'T CALL US WE'LL CALL YOU.

MOTIVATE CHILDREN WITH PRAISE

HOMEWORK WITH TEARS

HEY MOM, DAD!! GUESS WHAT! I GOT AN "A" ON MY HOMEWORK ASSIGNMENT! ISN'T THAT GREAT?!! ..... HELLO.... ... HELLO?!... EARTH TO PARENTS ...HELLLOOоо!!!

Children need encouragement and support from the people whose opinions they value the most—their parents. Your consistent praise can encourage your child to feel good about his or her ability *and* motivate your child to do his or her best work.

Each night praise your child about some specific accomplishment. Say something positive about a specific goal your child has set. Example: "I really like how you're doing your homework on your own now."

It is important to **PRAISE** all homework efforts. Let your child know just how proud you are of how hard he or she is working.

HOMEWORK WITHOUT TEARS

Use Super Praise to motivate your child!

First, one parent praises the child: "I really appreciate how hard you're working to do your homework. You finished it all during Daily Homework Time and you did a great job. I want to make sure Dad hears about this when he gets home."

Second, this parent praises the child in front of the other parent: "Patty did a really fine job on her homework today. She started it without complaining, she stayed with it, and she did a super job on it."

Finally, the other parent praises the child: "I really feel proud of you, getting such a good report from Mom. You're really doing fine!"

If you're a single parent, you can use a grandparent, a neighbor, or a family friend as your partner in delivering Super Praise. Any adult whose approval your children will value can fill the role of the second person offering praise.

USE A LONG-RANGE PLANNER

Long-range projects, with their due dates sometime in the "distant" future, are usually the most difficult assignments children receive in school. A Long-Range Planner can teach your child how to successfully complete longer projects. By using the Long-Range Planner, your child will learn how to break down a big, overwhelming project into small, easily completed tasks, each with its own "mini-deadline." Your child will also learn how to distribute the assignment over the period of time given for the project.

Assure your child that you will help him or her plan long-range projects in advance, but not at the last minute.

PRAISE your child for each mini-deadline that is met.

Agree with your child that he or she will inform you of all long-range assignments when they are first assigned.

Go over the Long-Range Planner with your child. Talk about the importance of meeting each of the mini-deadlines, so that the final deadline can be handled on time and without panic.

If a mini-deadline arrives and your child has not completed the work, use your full parental authority to insist that it is done immediately.

Reward your child for completing a long-range project on time!

Homework Without Tears for Teachers

Positive Notes for Parents

Run off copies of these notes and keep them handy for use throughout the year.

HOMEWORK NEWS FLASH

Dear _____,

Thought you'd like to know

that _____

is doing a great job on

homework because

_____

_____

_____

_____

Signed

_____

Date

Dear _____,

HOORAY!

_____
Student's name

did a great job on homework today

because _____

_____

_____

_____

Signed

_____

Date

Positive Notes for Parents

Run off copies of these notes and keep them handy for use throughout the year.

HOMEWORK SUPERSTAR!

Dear _____,

Thought you'd like to know

that _____

is doing a great job on

homework because

_____

_____

_____

_____

Signed

_____

Date

_____

HOMEWORK NEWS

PARENT RESOURCE SHEETS

When there is a homework-related problem you need help with, contact the parents by phone or in a face-to-face meeting.

With the parents discuss the problem the child is having with homework, e.g., takes all night to get it done, forgets to bring assignments home, etc.

Select the appropriate resource sheet and go over each of the steps to make sure the parent understands what is to be done. Then give or send the sheet home to the parents. Don't give the resource sheet to parents if you feel they will be intimidated by it. Just make sure they understand the steps they are to follow.

Set a time (in a week or two) to follow up with the parents to determine whether the strategy has been effective or if further action is necessary.

Parent Resource Sheets:

Note: You are welcome to translate these pages into any language appropriate for your parents.

For the parent(s) of _____

Homework is an excellent way to teach your child the importance of starting, sticking with and completing a job. It is also an opportunity to teach your child to do the best work he or she can. But your child may rush through homework in order to play, talk on the phone, watch TV, etc. You need to let your child know that doing homework and doing it well is a responsibility. Letting your child rush through an assignment or do sloppy work is teaching that it is all right not to do his or her best work.

Here's what to do when children don't do their best work:

1 Tell your child what you expect.

"I have been looking at your homework assignments and I know you can do a better job. You are not to rush through your assignments. I want you to take your time and do the best work you can. Sloppy work with a lot of mistakes is not acceptable."

2 Praise your child when he or she does good work.

Simply telling your child what you expect may be enough to inspire better work. If so, your child is doing better work *for you* and you need to be there to recognize it. After you have talked with your child, check the very next assignment. If the work is better, praise the effort by saying things like, "Great job getting your homework done," or, "I like how neat your work is today. Keep up the good work." Praising your child for good work is the best way to encourage continued best efforts.

3 Institute Mandatory Homework Time.

If your child still rushes through homework, it is probably because the faster it is done the more time he or she will have to play or watch TV. Mandatory Homework Time takes away these advantages of getting homework done as fast as possible.

Mandatory Homework Time means that a child must use the entire scheduled Daily Homework Time for homework or other academic activities *whether or not homework is completed*. In other words, if an hour is allotted each night (7:00 p.m.—8:00 p.m., for instance), the entire hour must be spent on homework. If homework is finished, the rest of the time must be spent on other academic work such as reading, reviewing textbooks or practicing math. When children learn that rushing through homework will not be rewarded with more free time, they will learn quickly to slow down and do a better job.

Continued on back

4   Provide additional incentives.

To encourage your child to continue good work, give a reward or a point toward a prize each time homework is completed. For instance, each night he or she does a good job on homework, one point is earned. When five points are earned the child is rewarded with an extra privilege.

5   If all else fails, contact the teacher.

If after trying the first four steps your child is still not doing his or her best work, contact the teacher. You and the teacher must work together to improve your child's performance.

KEEP THIS IN MIND: You cannot allow your child to be indifferent about homework. If your child learns that it is all right not to do his or her best work, that attitude can be carried outside of school to a job where a boss is much less sympathetic about sloppy work.

For the parent(s) of _____

When your child would rather battle with you every night rather than do homework, it is time to set firm limits. Your child may openly refuse to do homework or lie to you or to the teacher about why it hasn't been done. To solve this problem, you must make it clear to your child that choosing not to do homework is choosing not to enjoy certain privileges.

Here's what to do when children refuse to do homework assignments:

1 State clearly how you expect homework to be completed.

Tell your child, "I expect you to do all of your homework every night. Under no circumstances will I tolerate your refusing to do your homework assignments."

2 Back up your words with actions.

When your child is engaged in a power struggle with you and refuses to do homework, you must make it clear that his or her behavior will result in a loss of privileges. Tell your child: "You can choose either to do your homework or to not have privileges. If you choose not to do your homework, then, until you have finished your assignments, you will lose these privileges: You will not leave this house. You will not watch TV. You will not be allowed to listen to music or use the telephone. You will sit here until all of your homework is done. The choice is yours." Then, stick with your demands. It may take your child several days of sitting idly in his study area to realize that you mean business.

3 Praise your child when homework is done.

Praise your child each time he or she does homework. "I really like the way you've been getting your homework done. That's what I expect from you."

4 Use a Homework Contract to provide additional incentives.

A Homework Contract is an effective motivator for children of any age. It is an especially valuable tool because it encourages children to accept responsibility for an agreement made between you and your child. A Homework Contract is an agreement between you and your child that states: "When you do your homework, you will earn a reward." For example: "Each day that you bring home your homework and complete it during Daily Homework Time, you will earn one point. When you have earned five points, you may choose one night to stay up late." The younger the child, the more quickly he or she should be able to earn the reward.

Continued on back

5   If all else fails, contact the teacher.

With a very difficult child, contact the teacher and request that additional discipline be provided at school for homework assignments not completed. Your child will quickly learn that the school is backing up your efforts.

KEEP THIS IN MIND: Your child must learn that homework is not a battleground. There can be no power struggle over homework; it must be done. Your child must learn that conflict on this issue will not be tolerated.

For the parent(s) of _____

From time to time a child may forget to bring home books or homework assignments. But when your child *continually* fails to bring home assigned homework, you must take action.

Here's what to do when children fail to bring assignments home:

1 | **State clearly that you expect all homework assignments to be brought home.**

Tell your child, "I expect you to bring home all your assigned work and all the books you need to complete your assignments. If you finish your homework during free time at school, I expect you to bring it home so that I can see it."

2 | **Work with the teacher to make sure you know what homework has been assigned.**

Ask the teacher to have your child make a list of each day's homework assignments. The list is checked and signed by the teacher and brought home by your child. When your child completes the assignments, you sign the list and have your child return it to the teacher.

3 | **Provide praise and support when all homework assignments are brought home.**

Make sure that your child knows that you appreciate it every time he or she brings home all homework assignments. "It's great to see that you remembered to bring home all of your homework. I knew you could do it."

4 | **Institute Mandatory Homework Time.**

If your child still fails to bring home assignments, he or she may be avoiding homework time to play or watch TV. Mandatory Homework Time eliminates the advantages of forgetting homework. Mandatory Homework Time means that a child must use the entire scheduled Daily Homework Time for homework or other academic activities *whether homework is brought home or not*. In other words, if an hour is allotted each night (7:00 p.m—8:00 p.m., for instance), the entire hour must be spent on homework. If homework is not brought home, the entire time must be spent on other academic work such as reading, reviewing textbooks or practicing math. When children learn that their irresponsible approach to homework will not be rewarded with more free time, they will learn quickly to remember to bring home their assignments.

Continued on back

5 **Use a Homework Contract to provide additional incentives.**

A Homework Contract is an effective motivator for children of any age. It is an especially valuable tool because it encourages children to accept responsibility for an agreement made between you and your child. A Homework Contract is an agreement between you and your child that states: "When you do your homework, you will earn a reward." For example: "Each day that you bring home your homework and complete it during Daily Homework Time, you will earn one point. When you have earned five points, you may choose one night to stay up late." The younger the child, the more quickly he or she should be able to earn the reward.

6 **If all else fails, work with the teacher to follow through at school for homework not completed.**

If your child continues to forget homework, discuss with the teacher the possibility of imposing loss of privileges at school. Loss of recess or lunch time or after-school detention lets your child know that you and the school are working together to ensure that he or she behaves responsibly.

KEEP THIS IN MIND: Your child must learn to bring home and complete all homework assignments. Accept no excuses.

For the parent(s) of _____

Some children spend hours and hours on homework when it is really not necessary. They may stop and start and be easily distracted. When your child takes the entire evening to do homework, you need to step in and help solve the problem.

Here's what to do when children take all night to do homework:

1 State clearly that you expect all homework to be done during Daily Homework Time.

Tell your child: "I expect you to get all of your homework done during Daily Homework Time. Your taking all evening to do it must stop at once."

2 Make sure that homework is being done in a quiet study area.

Your child may take too much time to do homework because he or she is working in a distracting environment. Make sure that during Daily Homework Time your child has no access to TV, stereo, or other distractions and is not disturbed by brothers and sisters. You may wish to change the location of the study area if such distractions are present.

3 Provide praise and support when your child does homework on time.

Let your child feel your approval each time homework is finished during Daily Homework Time. "Great job! I am really pleased to see that you got your homework done on time. I'm so proud of you!"

4 Provide additional incentives when appropriate.

Your child may require additional help to develop the habit of getting homework done promptly. A good incentive for solving this particular problem is the Beat the Clock game. To play this game with your child, you first determine how long it should take for the child to finish the homework. Then at the start of Daily Homework Time, a timer (oven timer, alarm clock) is set. If the child finishes the homework appropriately within the given time, a special privilege is earned.

5 Back up your words with action.

If the first four steps do not succeed in getting your child to finish homework during Daily Homework Time, you must take a stand. Tell your child: "You have a choice. You can do your homework during Daily Homework Time or you can

Continued on back

choose not to have privileges. If you choose not to do your homework, then from the beginning of Daily Homework Time until you have finished your homework, you will lose these privileges: You will not leave this house. You will not watch TV. You will not be allowed to listen to music. You will not be allowed to use the telephone to either make or receive calls. You will sit there until your homework is finished. The choice is yours."

KEEP THIS IN MIND: Your child must learn to do homework responsibly and that there are limits to the help he or she can expect from you. Your child must learn to do homework efficiently, productively, and on time.

For the parent(s) of _____

If your child will not do homework without your assistance, you must make sure that he or she is making a genuine effort in trying to work alone. If your child insists that you sit with him or her all night or continually begs for your assistance, follow the steps below.

Here's what to do when children will not do homework on their own:

1 **State clearly that you expect your child to work alone.**

Tell your child: "I expect you to do your homework without my help. I will not sit with you or do your work for you. I will not be available to answer questions every five minutes."

2 **Provide praise and support when your child works on his or her own.**

Monitor your child during Daily Homework Time. When you see your child working alone, say: "I am really proud of the way you are doing all of this work on your own. I knew you could do it!" Be consistent with your praise.

3 **Help your child build confidence.**

Many children will not work without your help because they feel their homework assignments are just too much to handle on their own. "Chunking" is a great technique to help your child gain the confidence needed to work on his or her own. "Chunking" means dividing a big assignment into smaller chunks you know can be handled successfully. For example, a 20-problem math assignment would be broken into 5 chunks of 4 problems each. The child is rewarded with a prize (raisins, peanuts, etc.) each time one of the chunks is completed until the assignment is finished.

4 **Help your child only after he or she has genuinely tried to solve the problem on his or her own.**

Be sure that your child has tried the problem at least twice before you agree to help. There will be times when something is really too hard for your child to understand, but be sure that you don't step in until he or she has made a genuine effort to solve the problem.

5 **Provide additional incentives when appropriate.**

Another technique to help children learn to work on their own is "Trade-Off." With this game, place a bowl of small candies, raisins or peanuts in front of your

Continued on back

child and say: "Each time you ask me for help with your homework, you will have to give me one of these candies (raisins, etc.). When they are all gone, I won't help you anymore. At the end of Daily Homework Time, you get to keep what's left."

---

6 | Back up your words with action.

If the first five steps do not succeed in getting your child to work without your help, it is time to get tough. Make sure that your child knows that at the end of Daily Homework Time you will no longer be available to help and that your child will sit in his or her work space until the work is done—even if it means remaining there all evening. Be prepared for your child to use anger, tears or indifference to get you to back down. Let your child know that such tactics will not work and he or she will remain in the study area until he or she learns to work alone.

KEEP THIS IN MIND: Your child must learn to do homework on his or her own. Relying on you for help will only lead to greater dependence. Your child must develop the confidence to tackle any homework assignment on his or her own.

For the parent(s) of _____

If your child puts off starting long-range assignments until just before they are due, it can put stress on the entire family. Typically, this child waits until the last minute and then goes into a frenzy, demanding your immediate help. To solve this problem, you must take steps to teach your child about long-range planning.

Here's what to do when children wait until the last minute to finish assignments:

1 **State clearly that you expect long-range projects to be planned and completed responsibly.**

Sit down with your child and say that you will not tolerate putting off projects until just before they are due: "I expect you to plan your book reports (term papers, etc.) responsibly. This waiting until the last minute must stop."

2 **Ask the teacher for a Long-Range Planner.**

Ask your child's teacher to give your child a Long-Range Planner. By using the Long-Range Planner, your child will learn how to break down a large project into small, easily completed tasks and how to distribute the assignment over the period of time given for the project. Insist that your child tell you about each long-range assignment and then help your child use the planner to decide when each step of the project is to be completed.

3 **Provide praise and support for your child as each step is completed.**

Each time your child completes a step of a long-range project, express your approval: "I think that it is wonderful that you picked out the book for your report so quickly." "I really like how you finished reading the book before the date you scheduled! Keep up the good work."

4 **Provide additional motivators when appropriate.**

If your child needs additional motivation to complete a long-range project on time, institute a system that allows your child to earn a point toward a reward or privilege each time a step is completed according to the schedule.

5 **Back up your words with action.**

If the first four steps fail to motivate your child to do long-range planning, it's time to impose restrictions. If the child fails to read a book selected for a book report by the agreed-upon date, take away a privilege (playing outside, watching TV) until the book is read. Unless you set limits, your child is not going to believe that you mean business.

Continued on back

KEEP THIS IN MIND: Your child must learn to budget the time allocated for long-range projects. It's a skill that must be developed if your child is to be capable of taking on larger tasks as he or she grows up.

For the parent(s) of _____

If your child will not do homework unless there is a parent at home, you must take steps to help your child develop a more responsible approach to homework.

Here's what to do when children will not do homework if you're not home:

1 | **State clearly that you expect homework to be done whether you are home or not.**

Tell your child: "I expect you to get your homework done every night whether or not I am home."

2 | **Make sure that the person responsible for child care knows about Daily Homework Time.**

Make sure that the person responsible for your child's care knows where your child is expected to do homework (in the study area), when homework is to be done (during Daily Homework Time—which should be posted) and how your child is to do it (on his or her own). It is a good idea to sit down with your child and the caregiver and communicate your expectation that homework will be done just as though you were home.

3 | **Monitor your child when you're not home to make sure homework is done.**

Telephone your child at the beginning of Daily Homework Time to be sure homework has begun. Call back, if possible, at the end of Daily Homework Time to make sure your child has completed the assignments. Have your child leave completed homework out for you to check when you get home. You may phase out this monitoring as your child begins to work responsibly.

4 | **Provide praise and positive support.**

Praise your child for homework done in your absence. When you call at the start of Daily Homework Time and find that your child has started on time, say: "I really like the way you got started so promptly, even without my being there." When you get home and find homework completed, tell your child: "Great! You are doing such a good job on your homework when I am not here. Keep up the good work!"

5 | **Use additional incentives when appropriate.**

Special incentives may be necessary at first to get your child into the habit of doing homework without your supervision. A Homework Contract is an effective motivator that can work well with children of any age. It is an especially valuable tool because it encourages children to accept responsibility for an agreement made between them and their parents.

Continued on back

A Homework Contract states:

- That homework will be done whether you are home or not.
- The amount of time in which homework is to be completed.
- The number of points earned each time the child completes homework.
- The reward the child will receive when a certain number of points are earned.

For example, a child might receive 1 point each night homework is completed. When 5 points are reached, a reward is earned. The younger the child, the more quickly the child should be able to earn the reward. For grades 4-6, the contract should be in effect 1 to 2 weeks.

---

6 | Back up your words with action.

If the first five steps do not work, tell your child that he or she is required to sit in the study area until homework is finished, whether you are home or not. Tell the child: "You have a choice. You can do your homework during Daily Homework Time or you can choose not to have privileges. If you choose not to do your homework, then from the beginning of Daily Homework Time until you have finished your homework, you will lose these privileges: You will not leave this house. You will not watch TV. You will not listen to music. You will sit there until homework is finished. The choice is yours."

If there is no one providing child care, you may have to impose backup disciplinary consequences as soon as you get home. If you find homework not completed, turn off the TV, get your child off the phone, and make sure he or she gets back to work.

---

7 | If all else fails, work with the teacher to take action at school for homework not completed.

If your child continues to not complete homework, discuss with the teacher the possibility of imposing loss of privileges at school. Loss of recess or lunch time or after-school detention lets your child know that you and the school are working together to ensure that he or she behaves responsibly.

KEEP THIS IN MIND: Regardless of whether or not you're home, your child must realize that he or she is responsible for finishing all homework assignments. Your child must learn that irresponsibility about homework is unacceptable.

CREATIVE HOMEWORK MODEL WORKSHEETS

Pages 121-126 of the Appendix contain the reproducible worksheets for the Creative Homework Models presented in Chapter 7. Make one copy of each worksheet per student prior to giving the lesson.

Creative Homework Model Worksheets:

Homework Without Tears for Teachers

Name _____

Date _____

Interviewing for Information

Interview someone at home about _____
_____

Write down the information you learn in the space below.

Note: If you have a tape recorder, you might want to try recording your interview. Then play back the tape and write down the important information.

Name

Date

Sequencing

Draw or write the steps that show _____

Show _____ _____ steps.

Name _____

Date _____

Evaluating Different Opinions

In the conversation balloon to the left, write at least _____ reasons *for* the issue of

_____

_____

In the conversation balloon to the right, write at least_____ reasons *against* the same issue.

Name

Date

Imagining Yourself in Someone Else's Shoes

Imagine that you _____

_____

Write a diary page _____

Name _____

Date _____

Teach Your Parent Something That You Learned in School

Directions: Teach your parent three facts about _____
_____

Part One
Write the 3 three facts you are going to teach in the spaces below:

1 _____

2 _____

3 _____

Part Two
Plan how you are going to teach these three facts. Are you going to give an oral presentation, show charts or diagrams, read from a book. Will you ask your parent to take notes. In the space below, write how you will teach your lesson.

_____

_____

Part Three
Create three questions that will let you know whether or not your parent really learned the facts you taught. Use the spaces below to write your questions.

Question 1 _____

_____

Question 2 _____

_____

Question 3 _____

_____

Copy these questions on the back of this worksheet. This will be your parent's test!

Part Four
Teach your lesson, then give your parent the test questions written on the back of this worksheet.

Name _____

Date _____

Using Found Objects to Make a Model of Something Learned

Use small objects you find around your home to make _____
_____
_____

Write ideas below to help plan your project.

Objects I have found to use: _____
_____
_____
_____

What else I'll need: _____

How I will make my objects hold together: (Circle one or more.)

brads   clips   glue   paste   rubber bands

staples   string   tacks   other _____

What I like best about how I have used my found objects:
_____
_____
_____

What I will name my project: _____
_____

My child has permission to use the objects he or she has found to make a project for school.

Parent signature _____

RECOMMENDED READING

For readers desiring more information about homework, the following works are recommended for the subject areas listed below.

ACADEMIC ACHIEVEMENT

Fredrick, W.C., & Walberg, H.J. (1980). Learning as a function of time. *Journal of Educational Research, 73,* 183-204.

Keith, T. (1986). *Homework.* West Lafayette, IN.: Kappa Delta Pi.

Lavin, D.E. (1965). *The prediction of academic performance.* New York: Russell Sage Foundation.

EFFECTIVENESS AT THE ELEMENTARY SCHOOL LEVEL

Doane, B.S. (1973). The effects of homework and locus-of-control on arithmetic skills achievement in fourth-grade students. *Dissertation Abstracts International, 33,* 5548A.

Harnischfeger, A. (1980). Curricular control and learning time: District policy, teacher strategy, and pupil choice. *Educational Evaluation and Policy Analysis, 2 (6),* 19-30.

Hudson, J.A. (1966). A pilot study of the influence of homework in seventh grade mathematics and attitudes toward homework in the Fayetteville public schools. *Dissertation Abstracts International, 26,* 906.

Koch, E.A. (1965). Homework in arithmetic. *The Arithmetic Teacher, 12,* 9-13.

Levine,V. & Worley, W.R. (1985, April). *The impact of television and homework time on cognitive and noncognitive outcomes.* Paper presented at the annual meeting of the American Educational Research Association, Chicago.
Maertens, N., & Johnston J. (1972). Effects of arithmetic homework upon the attitude and achievement of fourth, fifth, and sixth grade pupils. *School Science and Mathematics, 72,* 117-126.

Paschal, R.A., Weinstein, T., & Walberg, H.J. (1984). The effects of homework on learning: A quantitative synthesis. *Journal of Educational Research, 78,* 97-104.

Stanley, J.C. (1980). Manipulate important educational variables. *Educational Psychologist, 15,* 164-171.

Wolf, R.M. (1979). Achievement in the United States. In H.J. Walberg (Ed.), *Educational environments and effects: Evaluation, policy, productivity.* Berkeley, CA.: McCutchan.

EFFECTIVENESS FOR HIGH AND LOW ACHIEVERS

Keith, T.Z. (1982). Time spent on homework and high school grades: A large-sample path analysis. *Journal of Educational Psychology, 74,* 248-253.

Stanley, op. cit.

EFFECTIVENESS AT THE HIGH SCHOOL LEVEL

Coleman, J.S., Hoffer, T., & Kilgore, S. (1981). *Public and private schools.* Washington, D.C.: U.S. Department of Education.

Foyle, H.C. (1984). The effects of preparation and practice homework on student achievement in tenth-grade American history. (Doctoral dissertation, Kansas State University, 1984). *Dissertation Abstracts International.*

Keith, T.Z. (1982). op. cit.

Keith, T.Z., & Page, E.B. (1985). Homework works at school: National evidence for policy changes. *School Psychology Review, 14.*

GRADED VERSUS NON-GRADED

Paschal, et. al., op. cit.

AS A MEANS TO INDIVIDUALIZE INSTRUCTION

Bradley, R.M. (1967). An experimental study of individualized versus blanket-type homework assignments in elementary school mathematics. *Dissertation Abstracts International, 28,* 3874a.

Check, J.F., (1966). Homework: Is It needed? *The Clearing House, 41,* 143-147.

QUALITY VERSUS QUANTITY

Leonard, M.H. (1965). An experimental study of homework at the intermediate-grade level. *Dissertation Abstracts International, 26,* 3782.

PARENTAL INVOLVEMENT

Epstein, J.L. (1984, April). *Effects of teacher practices of parent involvement for change in student achievement in reading and math.* Paper presented at the annual meeting of the American Educational Research Association, New Orleans.

LaConte, R.T. (1981). *Homework as a learning experience.* Washington, D.C.: National Education Association.

Maertens & Johnston, op. cit.

Walberg, H.J. (1984). Improving the productivity of America's schools. *Educational Leadership, 41 (8),* 19-30.

HOMEWORK POLICIES

Keith, op. cit.

RESPONSIBILITY

Fiesen, C.D. (1978). *The results of surveys, questionnaires, and polls regarding homework.* Iowa City, IA.: University of Iowa.

Keith and Page, op. cit.

ADDITIONAL SUPPORT FOR YOUR HOMEWORK PROGRAM

HOMEWORK WITHOUT TEARS® BOOKS

Homework Without Tears - A Parent's Guide for Motivating Children to Do Homework and to Succeed in School

A practical book that educators can use to help parents end the nightly battle over homework. Parents learn how to take an active role in the homework process. **#CA1205 $7.95**

Homework Without Tears for Teachers, Grades 1-3

Teachers will use this comprehensive guide, designed specifically for younger students, to teach their students how to do homework. Contains homework policy guidelines, complete lesson plans, reproducible homework models and parent tip sheets. **#CA1211 $9.95**

Homework Without Tears Homework Organizer

This delightfully written and illustrated book helps students remember their assignments, organize their time, develop good study habits and track their progress. Recommended for grades 4-8.

#CA1223 $3.95

Homework Motivators

These clever reinforcers will encourage students to do their very best on all homework assignments. Includes bulletin board ideas, individual incentives, charts and awards. Recommended for grades 1-6.

#CA1225 $6.95

Creative Homework

Teachers can quickly create interesting and educational homework assignments that allow students to apply the skills they've learned that day. Reproducible models includes suggestions for use in many subject areas.

Grades 1-3	**#CA1231**	**$5.95**
Grades 4-6	**#CA1232**	**$5.95**

Order from your local school supply dealer.

HOMEWORK WITHOUT TEARS® WORKSHOP FOR PARENTS

One of Lee Canter's associates can travel to your school or district to conduct a 2 1/2-hour workshop. Parents will understand what their role is in the homework process and learn techniques to influence their children toward more productive study habits.

For more information on conducting a Homework Without Tears Workshop for Parents, call Lee Canter & Associates at (800)262-4347. In California, call (213)395-3221